Beyond Telling Ain't Fieldbook

Methods, Activities, and Tools for Effective Workplace Learning

Harold D. Stolovitch
Erica J. Keeps

> If no CD-ROM is included with this book, please go to
> www.astd.org/TellingAintTraining
> to download all handouts and other materials to your hard drive.

ASTD
WORKPLACE LEARNING & PERFORMANCE
PRESS

Alexandria, VA

14   13   12   11   7   8   9

ASTD Press is an internationally renowned source of insightful and practical information on workplace learning and performance topics, including training basics, evaluation and return-on-investment (ROI), instructional systems development (ISD), e-learning, leadership, and career development.

Ordering information: Books published by ASTD Press can be purchased by visiting our Website at store.astd.org or by calling 800.628.2783 or 703.683.8100.

Library of Congress Control Number: 2004116272

ISBN-10: 1-56286-403-3
ISBN-13: 978-1-56286-403-3

Acquisitions and Development Editor: Mark Morrow
Copyeditor: Christine Cotting, UpperCase Publication Services, Ltd.
Interior Design and Production: Kathleen Schaner
Cover Design: Max Nigretto
Cover Illustration: Mark Shaver

Printed by Victor Graphics, Inc., Baltimore, Maryland, www.victorgraphics.com.

Table of Contents

Preface

Thank you for opening the covers of the *Beyond Telling Ain't Training Fieldbook* and turning to this page. You have given us an opportunity to express our delight and joy at how well the *Telling Ain't Training* book, itself, has been received. If sales and popularity are gauges of a book's success, then we have surpassed our modest expectations of adding to the already rich resources for learning professionals. The perspective of *Telling Ain't Training* was one of "learner advocate." The aim was to distance ourselves from the common practice of *transmitting information* and draw closer to the more effective approach of *transforming learners,* thus enabling them to perform in ways that they and the organizations and customers they serve all value.

It has been so much fun sharing our research, our many years of professional experience, and our views about workplace learning and performance in a practical, interactive, and challenging manner. We must have struck a chord somewhere, because as a result of *Telling Ain't Training*'s publication, the American Society for Training & Development (ASTD) launched a series of *Telling Ain't Training* mini-conferences in several American cities, all of which quickly sold out. ASTD has also received numerous requests to run workshops based on the book's contents. All in all, it has been exciting and incredibly rewarding to meet and work with trainers, instructional designers, communications specialists, human resource professionals, learning and performance support managers, organizational development specialists, and workplace and educational enthusiasts. All of them appear eager to make their learning investment yield higher returns than those they have been experiencing. All of the *Telling Ain't Training* events have been "happenings" in which participants have left fired up to make significant changes to current organizational practices or equipped with more ammunition to fight "learner-centered" battles they have been waging within their environments.

The preceding paragraph is the "good news." Despite this positive portrait, quite frankly there has been a decided performance gap. Yes, readers and conference and workshop participants have said wonderful things. However, they have also made it clear that *Telling Ain't Training* simply ain't enough. "The book is a great start," they tell us, "but we need something more. Give us materials and guidance on how we can move to action now. Give us something we can apply in our own organizations that is totally aligned with the *Telling Ain't Training* message."

We have listened . . . and heard. This *Beyond Telling Ain't Training Fieldbook* is our response. It takes each chapter of *Telling Ain't Training* and elaborates on it. It provides a large number of tools you can apply to bring the chapter content to life for you and your training organization.

The intended audiences for whom the *Fieldbook* has been created are training and performance improvement professionals who need support in their efforts to redirect their organizations from "telling and transmission" to "training and transformation"; occasional trainers, such as managers and supervisors who have some training responsibilities; subject-matter experts who are called on to train; training managers seeking higher rates of return on the training investment; and all other concerned workplace citizens who are convinced that their current training practices are insufficient.

Telling Ain't Training appears to have touched a nerve in the organizational training and development world. But it is only a book and, as earnestly as we tried to make it live the principles we were propounding, it still has largely "told" its message. This *Fieldbook* takes us several steps beyond *Telling Ain't Training*. It provides concrete actions and materials to transform telling into training. Please step over the threshold with us on another adventure.

We have divided the book into 14 chapters. Each chapter contains tools, techniques, and strategies to apply the principles of *Telling Ain't Training*. Starting with chapter 3, we briefly summarize (and sometimes comment on) the content from each of the *Telling Ain't Training* chapters. Most chapters conclude with a summary and encouragement to set in motion your transformation and that of your training organization.

Along the way you will encounter the following icons:

 This icon signals a reference to some part of *Telling Ain't Training*.

 This icon identifies key things you can do to transform yourself.

 This icon accompanies ideas for transforming your training organization.

Accompanying this *Fieldbook* is a CD-ROM that contains electronic copies of the assessments, exercises, exhibits, figures, tables, and worksheets that appear in the book.

These electronic documents are provided in PDF format so that you can display them in group training sessions or print copies to hand out to members of your training organization. To open or use these documents you will need Adobe Acrobat or Acrobat Reader software (which can be downloaded free of charge at www.adobe.com).

Before we conclude this preface and roll up our sleeves to dive into our work, please allow us to praise for a moment and sincerely thank the wonderful contributors to this *Fieldbook*.

Thank you, Mark Morrow, ASTD Acquisitions Editor, for encouraging and inspiring us to persist in the mission of supporting all those people who truly wish to transform wasted telling into valuable learning and performance. Mark initially set us on this journey and has accompanied us every step of the way.

No professional publication should ever see the light of day without a demanding, yet supportive, editor whose sole aim is to make your work the best it can be. Thank you, Christine Cotting, for helping us say it right and for defending the reader's/learner's right to a high-quality set of tools. You keep everyone honest.

Our sincerest thanks go out to Petti Van Rekom and Carol Goldsmith, who accepted the demanding task of reviewing what we produced and the doubly tough job of guiding us to make needed changes to the manuscript. These are professionals who undertook an onerous amount of work and whose only remuneration is our grumbling at having to rework something. Despite our groans at your perceptive suggested changes, we are grateful for your dedication to what is right for the user of this *Fieldbook*. Colleagues, we salute you.

Thank you, Jennifer Papineau, our graphic and technical support advisor. Every day you make us look better. You bring to life what we conceive.

Finally, there are no sufficient words to express our thanks to and acknowledgment of Samantha Greenhill. Regardless of what we dump on her—day, night, weekend, holiday—she simply responds, "No problem," and transforms our rough material into coherent manuscripts. Sam . . . you are wonderful!

We dedicate this *Fieldbook* to five of our clients—Alcan, DaimlerChrysler Academy, BBDO Detroit, The Coffee Bean & Tea Leaf, and Hewlett-Packard—for caring deeply about workplace learning and exhibiting leadership in this strategic arena.

As colleagues, friends, and life partners, we both enjoy sharing the knowledge and experience we have gained over the years not only with our professional community, but also with one another. Collaboratively, a publication requires constant, mutual support. Thank you, partner, for always being there.

Harold D. Stolovitch
Erica J. Keeps
Los Angeles, CA
May 2005

Introduction:
Why *Beyond Telling Ain't Training*?

This chapter

- ◆ reminds the reader that workplace training practices, even in our age of science, are still largely driven by myth
- ◆ reviews why it "ain't" always easy to do what is right
- ◆ suggests what it takes to "institutionalize" *Telling Ain't Training*'s recommendations
- ◆ states the mission and a promise for the *Beyond Telling Ain't Training Fieldbook.*

The message of the original *Telling Ain't Training* is simple and straightforward. To quote from chapter 1 of that book, "There are a lot of traditions, mythology and misguided—although well-intentioned—principles and activities in training that create barriers to effective learning. We have produced this book for two main reasons: to dispel these counterproductive beliefs and practices that harm the instructional process and to help you to be the most effective trainer/instructor you can be."

We continue to uphold our position about the vast amount of circulating nonsense that passes for training truisms (for example, "Tell them what you're going to tell them; tell them what you told them you would tell them; then, tell them what you've told them"). *Telling Ain't Training* refers to numerous "myths" throughout the book and even devotes an entire chapter (chapter 10) to dispelling some of these. It is the part about helping you "be the most effective trainer/instructor you can be" where we feel much more needs to be done than we originally estimated. The message of the book was easy enough to understand. It is in the application of what we provided that all the difficulties arise.

Why Ain't It Easy?

Why is it not so easy to do what is right? Why, if we know so much and are so convinced of what ought to be done, do we not just do it? Several reasons:

1. **Knowing ain't doing.** If you are like most people, you know what is appropriate to eat and what kind of and how much exercise you ought to engage in to remain healthy and fit. Hardly any of us could not prescribe a healthy regimen for another person. So why, as a society, are we so out of condition and overweight? Simple. Because knowing what is right does not mean we will do it.

   Telling Ain't Training, if its message was clear, has shown us what we ought to do to make every instructional activity meaningful, memorable, and transformable into worthwhile performance. Yet, as carefully explained and illustrated with examples as it is in chapters 3 and 4 of that book, acquiring declarative knowledge—the knowledge we have that enables us to name, explain, and talk about matters—is very different from procedural knowledge—knowledge that enables us to act and do things, to perform tasks. Again, to quote from *Telling Ain't Training,* "research on learning tells us that what we learn declaratively cannot be readily transformed into procedural knowledge . . . the reverse is also true." The bottom line is we know (declaratively) what ought to be done to make our training efforts more effective. It is just not an easy, straightforward thing to do it.

2. **Where do I start?** Newton's first law of motion states that objects at rest tend to remain at rest. The same applies to training practices within organizations. How does one get the ball rolling to overcome inertia? This is a reasonable question, particularly if you are not endowed with the power to command change (which does not always work, anyhow) or have special additional resources (unlikely in today's budget-stressed environment). The good news, as you will soon discover, is that *Beyond Telling Ain't Training* answers this question very practically.

3. **Can I do it alone?** No . . . yes . . . well, sort of. To explain, "no" is with respect to transforming your entire organization. Going it alone rarely accomplishes much, even if your intentions are worthy and you have a clear notion of what you wish to alter. As this *Fieldbook* suggests, you can start on your own and take certain initiatives. However, by involving others—colleagues, bosses, clients, and other specialists—you can accomplish enormous change. So, "yes" also fits. There are personal initiatives you can undertake that make a huge difference. Stand by for more on this as we proceed.

4. **How do I bring others aboard?** That's an excellent concern and question. The more the merrier . . . or at least the easier and more effective the evolution from telling to true training becomes. We have all learned that it is better to employ a team approach to implementing new ways of doing things than to

do it by oneself. We are highly sensitive to the need to get others involved. You are right to ask the question, and we promise not only answers but also tools and methods for doing this.

How Do I/We Institutionalize What *Telling Ain't Training* Recommends?

Institutionalization (quite a word) is what it's all about. We have seen initiatives fall by the wayside when the proponents—the evangelizers—move on before what they advocated takes root. *Telling ain't training* is a simple message, as is its mantra, "learner-centered . . . performance-based." Converting long-established practices (such as transfer-of-information sessions, cut-out-the-exercises-and-just-give-them-the-beef mentalities, or let's-do-a-Webcast scenarios) to saner, more effective transforming activities is far from simple. It takes planning, educating, and a host of in-your-face successes to capture all the stakeholders' attention and build different ways of thinking and acting. Once more, we hear you and will do our best to help you firmly plan, fertilize, and grow the changes you desire.

Let us leave this introductory chapter to find out what's in the *Beyond Telling Ain't Training Fieldbook* for you, and then you can move on to putting *Telling Ain't Training* into practice. We close with a statement and a promise:

Statement: The implied subtitle of *Telling Ain't Training* was "from transmission to transformation." This *Fieldbook*'s mission is to do just that.

Promise: We will turn over to you a number of tools, methods, guidelines, and activities that will speed up and anchor the transformation process. You and your training organization, if you follow our recommendations and use (or adapt) our tools, will change from *telling* to *effective training*.

That is a promise you can take with you to the chapters that follow.

Chapter 2

How the *Beyond Telling Ain't Training Fieldbook* Works

This chapter

- ◆ describes what is inside the rest of this *Fieldbook*
- ◆ provides an overview of how to get started using this *Fieldbook* and, incidentally, how to take a first step on the journey toward your and your training organization's transformation
- ◆ focuses attention on you and your training organization, and explains the importance of critical mass
- ◆ explains how you can put *Beyond Telling Ain't Training* to work.

Tools in this chapter include

- ◆ a *Telling Ain't Training* individual assessment that helps you determine where you are and where you want to be along seven *Telling Ain't Training* dimensions
- ◆ a *Telling Ain't Training* organization assessment that helps your training organization determine where it is and where it would like to be along seven *Telling Ain't Training* dimensions.

Essentially, this *Fieldbook* is your coach and guide. Chapter by chapter, it takes your hand and helps you put *Telling Ain't Training* to work for you and your training organization. Obviously, this means that you should have read *Telling Ain't Training* and have a copy handy as you proceed. If you can't fulfill these two conditions, stop right now, head over to your computer, and order a copy to be shipped immediately from www.astd.org. In the *Beyond Telling Ain't Training Fieldbook*, we frequently refer to content in the *Telling Ain't Training* book. We also frequently summarize some of the key points from that book's chapters and add comments on them.

Something Old . . .

In addition to the explanations, coaching, and guidelines, this *Fieldbook* contains a large number of tools, templates, examples, and recommendations for application.

We have drawn many of the tools from *Telling Ain't Training,* and have given them a fresh appearance or adapted them for your immediate use. These materials are yours to apply. Reproduce them, rework them for your environment, and disseminate them throughout your organization.

Something New...

We have created new, more extensive tools and systems expressly for this *Fieldbook.* They have all been tested in organizational settings and have demonstrated their worth. Here is a partial list of these additional materials:

- Instructions for designing learning games.
- Recipes and guidelines for developing case studies.
- A detailed methodology for debriefing experiential learning activities. This not only helps you draw out the most from learning events, but also converts what has been learned into direct workplace application.
- A detailed guide and system for conducting video-recorded practice training sessions. This easy-to-apply system comes complete with structured feedback forms and optional uses either as a stand-alone skill-building activity or as part of a train-the-trainer program for a new or existing course or curriculum.
- A CD-ROM containing all of the tools. This makes it easy for you or your training organization to print tools and templates for reuse, group learning sessions, and adaptation/customization for your environment.

Just as in *Telling Ain't Training,* this book presents specific aspects of training in each chapter. The chapters are not linked in a process flow. Rather, they work together to build a comprehensive portrait of training. Chapters 3 through 12 of this *Fieldbook* mirror *Telling Ain't Training* chapter by chapter. The final two chapters of *Beyond Telling Ain't Training* break new ground.

Assessing Yourself and Your Training Organization

Welcome to the first two tools of *Beyond Telling Ain't Training.* Because you are right at the beginning, it is appropriate for you to step on the scale, so to speak, and assess yourself as well as your training organization in two ways: where you currently are and where you want to be. Here is how the first two tools, Assessment 2-1: *Telling Ain't Training* Individual Evaluation and Assessment 2-2: *Telling Ain't Training* Organization Evaluation, work:

1. Notice that the same instrument seems to appear twice (Assessments 2-1 and 2-2). This is so that you can answer the first one for yourself—where you are and where you want to be—and answer the second according to where you believe your organization is and ought to be. For the second one, consider engaging the assistance of colleagues, customers, and/or your manager(s). The

Assessment 2-1: *Telling Ain't Training* Individual Evaluation

Dimension	State A	1	2	3	4	5	6	7	8	9	10	State Z
My mission	To transmit to learners information that is accurate, up-to-date, and complete											To transform learners so that they perform in ways that they and all stakeholders value
How I am viewed by management and clients	Primarily as a deliverer of content											Primarily as an agent of performance change
My basic job	Create and/or deliver content-accurate courses											Create individuals and/or teams able to demonstrate that they achieve what is expected of them
The products and services I provide	Courses and curriculum materials											Processes, tools and sufficient practice, feedback, follow-up, and support so that learners can perform back on the job
My needs-assessment process	Take training orders from management and/or customers											Verify where knowledge and skill gaps exist and identify where and what kind of training or other forms of support should be given
My evaluation practices	Check learners' reactions to and perceptions of the training											Verify learning, transfer of learning to the job, and impact of learning on bottom-line results
My accountabilities	How well learners rate my training/courses and how many were trained											How well learners perform on the job and my contribution to bottom-line results

Assessment 2-2: *Telling Ain't Training* Organization Evaluation

Dimension	State A	1	2	3	4	5	6	7	8	9	10	State Z
Our training organization's mission	To transmit to learners information that is accurate, up-to-date, and complete											To transform learners so that they perform in ways that they and all stakeholders value
How our training organization is viewed by management and clients	Primarily as a deliverer of content											Primarily as an agent of performance change
Our training organization's basic job	Create and/or deliver content-accurate courses											Create individuals and/or teams able to demonstrate that they achieve what is expected of them
The products and services our training organization provides	Courses and curriculum materials											Processes, tools and sufficient practice, feedback, follow-up, and support so that learners can perform back on the job
Our needs-assessment process	Take training orders from management and/or customers											Verify where knowledge and skill gaps exist and identify where and what kind of training or other forms of support should be given
Our evaluation practices	Check learners' reactions to and perceptions of the training											Verify learning, transfer of learning to the job, and impact of learning on bottom-line results
Our training organization's accountabilities	How well learners rate our training/courses and how many were trained											How well learners perform on the job and our contribution to bottom-line results

more people involved, the sooner and more effectively you can influence them. Also, it's good to understand that large discrepancies between how you assess yourself (both current and desired states) and how you assess your training organization should trigger some insights and cautions.

2. There are seven dimensions in both versions of this instrument. Follow the instructions for each of these to complete the assessments.

3. A difference of three or more points between your or the training organization's current and desired states on any dimension suggests that there is much to be done and that this *Fieldbook* will be helpful—as will a great deal of political will, effort, and support.

4. A difference of three or more points between how you rate your desired state on any dimension and the training organization's desired-state rating for that dimension clearly indicates that you will have to find allies, create success examples, and provide a lot of show-me practice and cases to help your organization evolve.

Assessments 2-1 and 2-2 are reusable and should be revisited on a regular basis to chart progress (every four months, for example). We will be presenting them again in the final chapter of this *Fieldbook,* just to see if there have been any changes since you started out on this venture.

An Activity for You

Here are the instructions for using Assessment 2-1: *Telling Ain't Training* Individual Evaluation:

1. For each dimension, read the descriptions at both ends of the continuum.

2. For each dimension, using two different colored pens or pencils, place an "X" on the continuum at those points you consider to be your own current state (one color) and your own desired state (the second color).

3. When you have placed all of your Xs in both colors, use a ruler to join all Xs in the "desired" color and then join all the Xs in the "current" color. You'll have two (probably zig-zag) vertical lines. Here is an example (current = solid line; desired = dashed line):

The greater the discrepancy between current and desired states for yourself or the organization, the more work you have cut out for you.

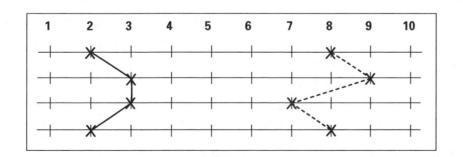

4. Note the discrepancies between the two zig-zag lines. A distance of three points or more between desired and current states on any dimension suggests that you have a lot to do to move from where you are to where you want to be.

An Activity for Your Training Organization

Here are the instructions for using Assessment 2-2: *Telling Ain't Training* Organization Evaluation:

The greater the discrepancy between where you are personally and where your organization is (especially with respect to the desired state), the more carefully you will have to proceed. A lot of "show-me" type of change management will be needed.

1. For each dimension, read the descriptions at both ends of the continuum.
2. For each dimension, using two different colored pens or pencils, place an "X" on the continuum at the point you think should be your training organization's desired state (one color) and at the point you consider to be your training organization's current state (the second color).
3. When you have placed all of your Xs in both colors, use a ruler to join the Xs in the "desired" color and then join all the Xs in the "current" color. Again you'll have two irregular vertical lines. Here's an example (current = solid line; desired = dashed line):

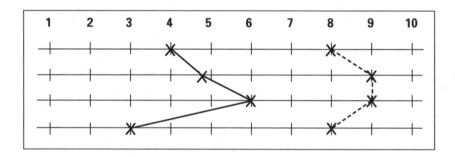

4. Note the discrepancies between the two zig-zag lines. A distance of three or more points between desired and current states suggests that your training organization has a lot to do to move from where it is to where it ought to be.

Focusing on You and Your Training Organization

Now that you have completed the two assessments, yours and your training organization's, you probably found a number of gaps between current and desired states. Closing these gaps requires thoughtful planning, resources, and effort. If your perceptions are radically different from those of your training organization, then you will have to add to your list of necessities strong willpower, commitment, allies, and political astuteness, as well as dexterity.

As we progress through this *Fieldbook,* we will offer assistance and recommendations for recruiting support. Right now we offer two strong suggestions:

1. **Work on yourself.** Before fixing anyone else or your training team/group/department, begin by clarifying your own goals. Build your own

"transforming" strengths. As you proceed, you will find that we have a lot for you to do. Do it. Learn from it, and increase your personal forces.

2. **Create a critical mass** of like-minded people to help change from telling to valuable training. In this *Fieldbook,* we give you a host of activities to help bring others onboard. Organize to make these happen. Reinforce those who participate. Reward all progress steps toward success.

Putting *Beyond Telling Ain't Training* to Work

This *Fieldbook* is not a *reading* book—it's a *doing* book, a resource for you to use and apply within your work context. You have reviewed the introduction, completed the assessments, and now have a sense of what has to be done. This naturally leads you to the next chapter and a familiar exercise from *Telling Ain't Training.* And there you'll find additional activities for you and your colleagues to carry out.

Chapter 3

Learning Is Not Easy

This chapter

- ◆ presents the discrepancies between what we know helps us learn and what we do when we step into the training role
- ◆ guides you and your training organization to align what helps learning with how you should train.

Tools in this chapter include

- ◆ I learn best when . . . —a worksheet that enables you and your training organization to identify what things help you take the steps to learn best and what things help you provide these for your learners.

There is a huge gap between how people say they learn—what helps them best to acquire new knowledge and skills—and how they are actually taught. What is true for ordinary, garden-variety learners is also true for teachers, trainers, coaches, instructors, and professors. As we pointed out in *Telling Ain't Training,* those who teach for a living can easily identify what best helps them learn. But when we go out to observe those self-same "educators" in action, we see almost a complete reversal between what people say about how they learn and how they try to help others learn.

In Worksheet 3-1 are some of the statements we use when we ask our teachers and trainers what helps them learn best. They are the same ones that appear in *Telling Ain't Training* (p. 7). However, we have added something extra to go beyond simply identifying what helps you (and by extension, others) learn best. We ask, "What must I do to change?"

An Activity for You

Please turn to Worksheet 3-1 and follow these directions. (We'll meet you at the other end when you have completed the activity.)

1. Columns A and B present sets of paired statements. Check off the statement in each pair that more closely corresponds to your personal, positive experience in learning. (Check only one in Column A or Column B each time.)
2. If the statement you checked is something you do not usually incorporate into your own method of instruction, check the box in the column whose heading is "I Don't Give My Learners Enough of This."
3. Finally, in the last column jot down at least one action you must take to ensure that your learners are appropriately engaged.
4. Check back and review what you have just done. Do you see any patterns emerging? Check off below the descriptions that fit your entries.

In my training,

- ☐ I tell too much.
- ☐ I don't emphasize what's in it for the learners.
- ☐ I show more than I involve.
- ☐ I don't include enough practice.
- ☐ Other: _____

If you listed actions to include more of what helps learners (who are just like you, for the most part) learn best, that's great!

An Activity for Your Training Organization

Now it is time to try this out with others in your training organization. Introduce Worksheet 3-1 in a friendly, supportive manner and at a convenient time. Here are some useful suggestions:

- ◆ Introduce the worksheet during a team meeting.
- ◆ Introduce it following information or comments on the "quality of our training."
- ◆ Send it via email, accompanied by a stimulating message, supported by the manager, and with a promise of results while maintaining individual confidentiality. When you have collected everyone's responses, synthesize these either in a brief summary or, informally, during a meeting.
- ◆ Debrief the worksheet activity by discussing similarities and differences in proposed actions.
- ◆ Identify high-probability-of-success changes that transform telling into training.
- ◆ Set up a challenge to yourself and the entire group. Select a training program you have delivered before. Based on "Actions I Can Take to Change" entries, prescribe specific changes to the program. Do this on your own. Also, have the whole group do this as an exercise using an excerpt from a training program.
- ◆ Debrief the exercise with a colleague whose judgment you respect or with your manager, if you have done it alone.

Worksheet 3-1: I Learn Best When . . .

Column A	Column B	I Don't Give My Learners Enough of This	Actions I Can Take to Change
☐ Someone who knows something I don't know explains and describes it to me.	☐ I discuss a topic with someone who knows something I don't know.	☐	
☐ I observe a demonstration.	☐ I get involved and try things out during a demonstration.	☐	
☐ I attend lectures at which an instructor presents information to me.	☐ I attend sessions at which an instructor engages me in a two-way interaction.	☐	
☐ I see what's in it for the organization.	☐ I see what's in it for me.	☐	
☐ There is a lot of detailed content.	☐ There is minimal, but meaningful, content.	☐	
☐ What is presented to me is organized according to the logic of the content.	☐ What is presented to me is organized according to the logic of how I learn.	☐	
☐ I am shown how things are done.	☐ I get to try things for myself.	☐	
☐ I attend long learning sessions.	☐ I attend short learning sessions.	☐	
☐ I am in a formal instructional setting.	☐ I am in an informal work and learning session.	☐	
☐ I am told how things work.	☐ I experience how things work.	☐	
☐ I listen and memorize.	☐ I practice.	☐	

◆ Debrief the exercise with the whole group if you had all of them involved. Draw conclusions about the prescribed changes. Emphasize how this will improve the quality and effectiveness of the training and learning.

Worksheet 3-2 is an example of Worksheet 3-1 filled in by a training team working with Lightning Electronics. The example includes prescribed changes to a sample training program. We have included some debriefing notes. Use the Lightning Electronics case study as a model for an activity or adapt it to match your organizational content.

Case Study: Lightning Electronics

Background: Lightning Electronics is a retailer of consumer electronic products. Its target market comprises home and small-business/office users. Its image is that of a store with good-quality products at great prices. It also tries to project an image of "customer consulting," not just selling. One of its high-volume items is printers, especially inexpensive name-brand models.

Lightning Electronics has 40 stores located in four contiguous western states. It hires highly motivated, younger people in their final years of college or new university graduates. It pays its sales consultants slightly more than the going rate and provides bonuses based on sales volume and revenues generated. In addition, it offers incentives for selling particular items.

Training: Most of Lightning Electronics' training is in the form of in-store or regional face-to-face training. A corporate trainer or a vendor trainer usually runs the sessions with anywhere from 12 to 30 participants. Training generally lasts two to three-and-a-half hours. Most of the sessions focus on product training: features, benefits, technical specifications, market positioning, warranties, and competitive-edge characteristics. Essentially, the training is in lecture format with projected visuals, a lot of information, product data sheets, and some hands-on practice (if enough products are available and time permits).

Training seems to be adequate. Participants listen. There are usually very few questions. However, informally and from "mystery shop" reports, sales consultants are often found to be weak with respect to identifying customer needs, answering user-type questions, offering alternatives when the customer is uncertain, and doing add-on suggestion selling. They are best in situations in which the customer asks for a particular item and they can show it and ring up the sale.

Synthesis of Worksheet Responses

Here are the patterns the Lightning Electronics respondents checked off:

- ☒ I tell too much.
- ☒ I don't emphasize what's in it for the learners.
- ☒ I show more than I involve.
- ☒ I don't include enough practice.
- ☒ Other: I don't provide enough job-related scenarios and selling practice.

Here is a summary of the debriefing notes—what emerged from the debriefing:

- There was high consensus among the six members of the training team that there is too much "telling" and that the product training is not contextualized. It is not

Worksheet 3-2: I Learn Best When . . . Example from Lightning Electronics

Column A	Column B	I Don't Give My Learners Enough of This	Actions I Can Take to Change
☐ Someone who knows something I don't know explains and describes it to me.	☒ I discuss a topic with someone who knows something I don't know.	☒	• Ask questions of participants • Ask about customers who might want/need targeted products
☐ I observe a demonstration.	☒ I get involved and try things out during a demonstration.	☒	• Have a few participants try out and demo products to the group
☐ I attend lectures at which an instructor presents information to me.	☒ I attend sessions at which an instructor engages me in a two-way interaction.	☒	• Create customer scenarios and have participants match customers with products • Question what triggered match choices
☐ I see what's in it for the organization.	☒ I see what's in it for me.	☒	• Stress benefits to sales consultants: satisfied customers, low returns, bonuses
☐ There is a lot of detailed content.	☒ There is minimal, but meaningful, content.	☒	• Decrease content • Focus on essentials • Provide clear job aids
☐ What is presented to me is organized according to the logic of the content.	☒ What is presented to me is organized according to the logic of how I learn.	☒	• Present products in a sales setting with scenarios and dialogue
☐ I am shown how things are done.	☒ I get to try things for myself.	☒	• Set up products and job aids • Leave lots of time for hands-on practice and role play
☐ I attend long learning sessions.	☒ I attend short learning sessions.	☒	• Time is adequate. Just give the participants more to do within the time frame.
☐ I am in a formal instructional setting.	☒ I am in an informal work and learning session.	☒	• Reduce psychological distance between trainer and participants • Create role plays and set up as in a store
☐ I am told how things work.	☒ I experience how things work.	☒	• Encourage questions and reward them. Have other participants find answers.
☐ I listen and memorize.	☒ I practice.	☒	• Provide in-class practice in selling • Provide scenarios and create buddy teams to practice back on the job

presented from a sales perspective and focuses almost exclusively on product specifications.

- Changes that are highly likely to transform telling to training include increased interaction, drawing from participant experience; scenario-based examples; role plays; job aids to be tried in class and used back on the job; less-detailed content; a focus on key customer profiles and needs; and in-class and in-store practice.
- Based on the synthesis and debriefing, each training specialist will take one product knowledge course and integrate the suggested changes within two weeks. A show-and-tell with brief demonstration will be included in the next monthly meeting.

Chapter Summary

You had a lot to do in this chapter. Here's a short recap:

- ◆ You revisited the "I learn best when . . . " exercise from *Telling Ain't Training*, but this time you moved from just making choices about how you learn best to "how I can change this into actions for my learners."
- ◆ You reviewed a model for doing the exercise for yourself and with your group.
- ◆ You examined debriefing recommendations for the "I learn best when . . . " exercise that allows you to synthesize your and your group's responses and then to transform these into actions with real training sessions.
- ◆ You visited the Lightning Electronics example and saw what emerged and what they decided to do.

So . . .

It's now your turn. Complete Worksheet 3-1 yourself. Have your team do it. Synthesize. Debrief. Move to action.

Then, proceed to the next chapter to review and apply some familiar training terms.

Chapter 4

An Introduction to Some Familiar Terms

This chapter

- ◆ reviews four key training terms, emphasizing their meanings and application to workplace learning
- ◆ restates the trainer's mantra from *Telling Ain't Training*, but now makes it operational with tools
- ◆ introduces task analysis as the key to ensuring that your training truly is performance based.

Tools in this chapter include

- ◆ a learner-centered preparation worksheet to guide you in developing learner-centered training
- ◆ a task-analysis checklist to help you ensure that your task analysis is complete and correct.

In chapter 2 of *Telling Ain't Training* we introduced you to a few key "training" terms. Let's see what you remember because these are important for you to recall and share with others.

Match meanings to terms in the exercise below by writing the letter of the meaning next to the term it defines:

Term	Meaning
1. _____ Training	A. Change in mental structures that leads to the potential for behavior change.
2. _____ Instruction	B. Activity whose purpose is to create a change in learners so that they consistently reproduce the same behaviors without variation, and do so increasingly more accurately and automatically.
3. _____ Education	C. The result of a variety of life experiences and highly generalized learning principles and events. Its purpose is to build general mental models and value systems.
4. _____ Learning	D. Activities that help learners generalize beyond the specifics of what is taught.

The correct responses are 1-B, 2-D, 3-C, and 4-A.

Please remember that training, instruction, and education are all valid and valuable means for creating learning. Each has its reason for existing. If you still feel a bit fuzzy about these terms, return to pages 9–13 in *Telling Ain't Training* for a quick refresher. You may even want to pull out the exercises related to these terms and introduce them to your training organization, group, or team, with a suitable debriefing. Here is a succinct way for you to tie all of the terms together:

> . . . training, instruction, and education all aim at building knowledge and skills in learners. Each offers a unique and distinct approach, and all are necessary to help people learn. They seldom remain "pure." They can be mixed so that even while training for a specific behavior, we may be educating by attitude and by the example we create for our learners.

Learner-Centered . . . Performance-Based: The *Telling Ain't Training* Mantra

We now proceed from terms to application of the terms. Remember, our mantra in *Telling Ain't Training* is "learner-centered . . . performance-based." The words are wonderful, but how do you make sure that you live this mantra in your work?

Let us return to each part of the mantra and the scenarios from *Telling Ain't Training* (pages 13 and 14) to bring it to life.

Learner-Centered Training

Let's now consider two activities—one for you and one for your training organization. Review the first exercise, checking off your choice: A or B. Then direct your colleagues' attention to a helpful checklist.

An Activity for You

Imagine that you are an accountant and have been asked to run a training session next week for a group of technical and professional personnel recently promoted to managers. Your mandate is to teach cash flow management to these non-financial managers. What will you do to prepare? Be honest and check off which of the following two scenarios more closely describes actions you would take.

☐ **A.** Gather materials on cash flow management. Examine documents for key concepts and terms. Create an outline of the content in logical sequence so that you ensure you hit all the fundamentals. Study up and rehearse so that you appear credible and can answer any content questions the learners raise. Put together information and exercises that clarify what cash flow is and how it works. Verify that all of your content is accurate and state-of-the-art.

☐ **B.** Gather information on the prospective learners' jobs with respect to cash flow. Gather information on the learners' backgrounds and experiences concerning cash flow management. Investigate to identify problems new managers encounter and create with respect to cash flow. Gather a list of organizational expectations of these newly appointed managers concerning cash flow management. Create realistic scenarios and tools to help the learners acquire expected competencies. Create a list of benefits to them and to the organization when they manage cash flow well.

By now, you know what the right response is (that is, B). Preparation to ensure that your training is truly learner-centered is key. So, based on the previous exercise, we can now create a preparation checklist (Worksheet 4-1). Use this checklist to guide your preparation in making your training learner-centered.

Worksheet 4-1: Preparation Checklist

- ☐ Gather information on your prospective learners' jobs, focusing on what they are expected to learn.

- ☐ Gather information on the learners' backgrounds and experiences, relative to what they are expected to learn.

- ☐ Investigate to identify problems your targeted learners encounter when they either try to do what is in their training during a session or when they return from training and try to apply what they have learned.

- ☐ Gather a list of organizational expectations with respect to how your learners are supposed to perform when they have been trained.

- ☐ Create realistic scenarios and tools to help learners acquire the capability to perform during training and back on the job.

- ☐ Create a list of benefits to learners and to the organization that result from the training.

An Activity for Your Training Organization

Introduce the checklist (Worksheet 4-1) after doing the previously presented cash flow exercise with your colleagues. It works well with individuals assigned to a new training task or as a group endeavor with your entire team. Develop a strategy for making all training learner-centered. Here is a starter list for such a strategy. Build on it. Enrich it and integrate it into the "way we normally do our work."

Learner-Centered Strategy Starter List
- Whenever we are asked to develop or deliver training, we ask, "What triggered this request?" We determine what the business need is that caused the request.
- We identify all targeted learner audiences and their characteristics related to the training request (more on this in chapter 5). These characteristics include

  — projected number of learners

  — educational and work background and experience

  — aptitudes and experience relative to the request

  — attitudes toward the desired knowledge and skills they are expected to acquire from the training

  — actual or potential misconceptions regarding what they are expected to learn

  — learning methods and language preferences

  — actual or potential obstacles or barriers to their learning and then applying the learning to the job.

- We focus on developing training that is relevant to the learners' job tasks and on what they can apply.
- We create processes, procedures, tools, and job aids that they learn to apply during training.

- During training we focus more on practice and feedback than on content presentation.
- We focus on transfer to the job and on post-training learner success.
- We emphasize the benefits of the training to learners.
- We inform our clients and management of learner success.
- We create tools and support systems for supervisors to encourage learners prior to training and to coach them when they return from training.
- [Add your own.]

Performance-Based Training

The key to a performance-based approach to training is to focus on what the learner is supposed to be able to do as a result of your training. From the two choices below, check the one that is consistent with a performance-based philosophy:

☐ **A.** They should be aware of the technical specifications of each item in the newly released product line.

☐ **B.** They should be able to match the right product from our new product line to the customer's need and demonstrate with concrete examples the benefits of the selected product in terms the customer understands.

B is the only acceptable choice. It states what performance the learner must demonstrate. It is job relevant and readily verifiable. We are very uncomfortable with the term *awareness training*. If we could have our way, we would delete it from your and your training organization's vocabulary database.

How can you ensure that your training will always be performance-based? By conducting a task analysis prior to developing any training. Let's see what we mean by this, using a simple case.

Case: Pack It Right

The request for training originated with the vice president of marketing and sales. She had been noticing over the past year that a number of sales representatives had been showing up to business meetings not looking crisp and professional. Moreover, she had observed first-hand in her travels that some of the sales reps obviously had no idea how to properly pack for a trip. The vice president felt that, given their industry—hospitality—properly packing for a business trip was an essential skill for sales and marketing representatives. Her expectation was that everyone should be able to select an appropriate suitcase, decide what should go into it for a given trip, and organize the contents so that everything is there when needed—and nothing is wrinkled or reeking of cologne. She expected her teams to turn up at all client meetings clean, crisp, professional, and confident.

Take 1: Preparing Training the Usual Way

The training specialist worked with a subject-matter expert (SME), a former manager of flight attendants for an airline, and came up with a brief "training session" that contained a number of projection slides with text. The slides showed suitcases poorly and well packed with accompanying text. There were also some humorous slides (such as one showing a sales rep pulling out a rumpled suit obviously covered with spilled cologne).

The session was well received by the sales and marketing representatives. Expressions such as these were heard as participants left the training: "cute"; "fun"; and "a waste of 90 minutes, but I guess I should pack better." Overall, reactions were fairly positive. The vice president pointed out, however, that several weeks later nothing much had changed.

Take 2: Preparing Training From a Performance-Based Perspective

The training specialist worked with an SME, a former manager of flight attendants for an airline. He had the expert demonstrate how to pack a suitcase properly, and he asked numerous probing questions as the expert explained and performed. Using sticky-notes on a large whiteboard, the training specialist began with the overall desired sales and marketing rep performance outcome:

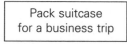

After listening to the SME talk about the main "things you have to do," he interrupted, asking, "If the sales or marketing rep does this [see figure below] perfectly, would he accomplish the overall task?"

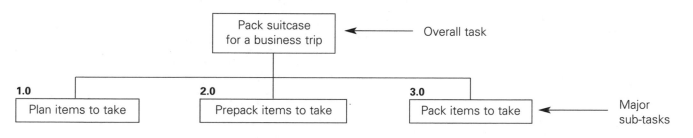

"Yes," the SME replied, "if he can do each of these perfectly and follow guidelines, it will add up to accomplishing the overall task."

Eventually what emerged was the task analysis presented in Exhibit 4-1 on page 24.

Notice that the task analysis emphasizes what it is that the learner must do to achieve overall success. The task analysis

- is learner-centered. It states what the learner must do to perform as required.
- does not concern itself with teaching, training, or instructing. It is strictly focused on learner performance with respect to the job requirement (in this case, properly packing a suitcase for a business trip).

Let us examine another case and then send you and your colleagues off to do a task analysis on your own.

Case: Conduct a Hiring Interview

The request for training originated with the director of human resources development, at the instigation of the company president. Given the climate of change in the company—increased competition and greater customer focus—senior

Exhibit 4-1

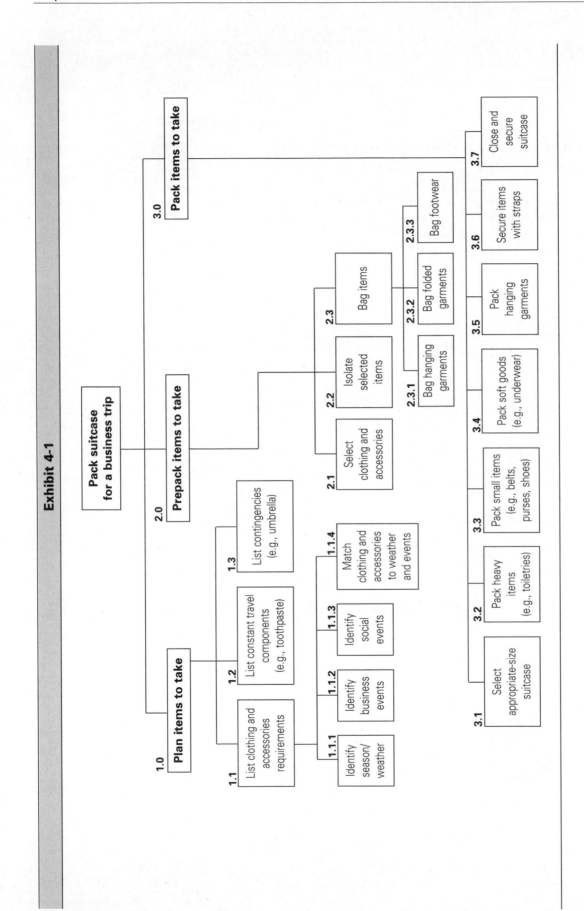

management was concerned with the nature and character of the current, remaining employee base following a serious workforce reduction. The feeling was that the majority of retained employees were not agents of change. Senior management wanted "fresh blood." In the past, people had been hired for specific jobs. The result: They could perform as required, but were not necessarily promotable. Senior management came to believe that employees must possess skills and characteristics for the future, and they targeted 40 key managers who had been with the company for a number of years and who they considered to be good mentors. These managers understood the company and its needs. Senior management wanted this group to become actively involved in interviewing and selecting a new breed of employee with the "right stuff."

The training specialist worked with three subject-matter specialists, including the director of human resource development, who dropped in from time to time to review progress and contribute ideas. What emerged was the task analysis depicted in Exhibits 4-2, 4-3, and 4-4 (pages 26–28).

Notice that the task analysis in the second case is more detailed than the one for "Pack a Suitcase." Nevertheless, it follows exactly the same rules.

Task-Analysis Tips

Here are some tips to help you conduct successful task analyses:

1. Create a compatible task-analysis team that includes SMEs who really know how to do the job. Whether you are developing a learning program to diagnose technical breakdowns, plan a sales campaign, demonstrate a new product, or analyze a profit-and-loss sheet, this principle remains the same. Also identify other experts who can review and verify what you and your team produce.

2. Your main job is to be the learner's advocate. Repeatedly ask the question, "What must the learner be able to do?" Whether the answer is name features of the XYZ system, describe the functioning of a pressure gauge, or extract a molar, the result must be observable and/or measurable. The best term to use is *verifiable*.

3. Sometimes you are given SMEs who don't have all of the information you need to complete an accurate task analysis. They may not be sufficiently knowledgeable or experienced in the content area, or the content may be new and evolving. Establish right up-front that they should inform you of their uncertainties. Ask them to identify people or materials that can provide missing pieces. If there is no single source of correct information—especially true in the case of evolving systems and technologies—create hypotheses and note these as such for later verification. Have other experts review what you have produced. Build consensus on what is most probably correct. Keep in mind that you can always return to your task analysis and modify it as new information becomes available.

Exhibit 4-2

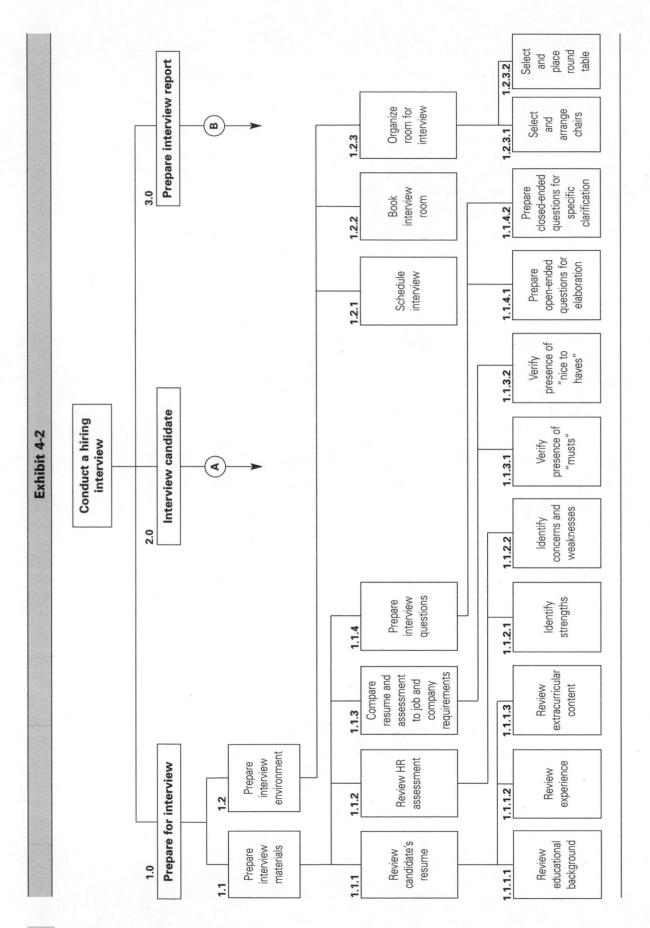

Exhibit 4-3

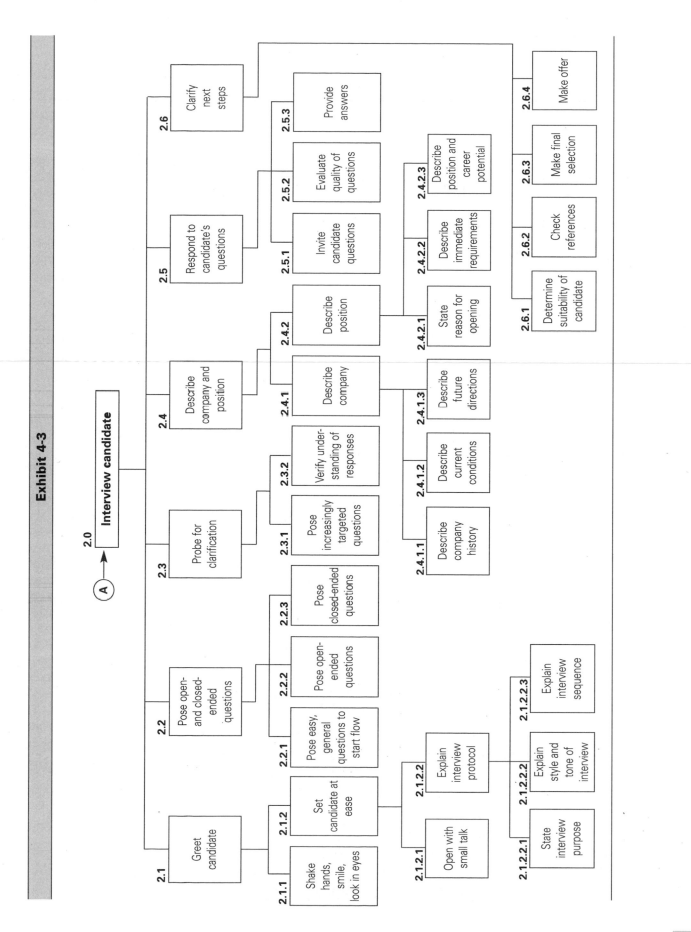

Exhibit 4-4

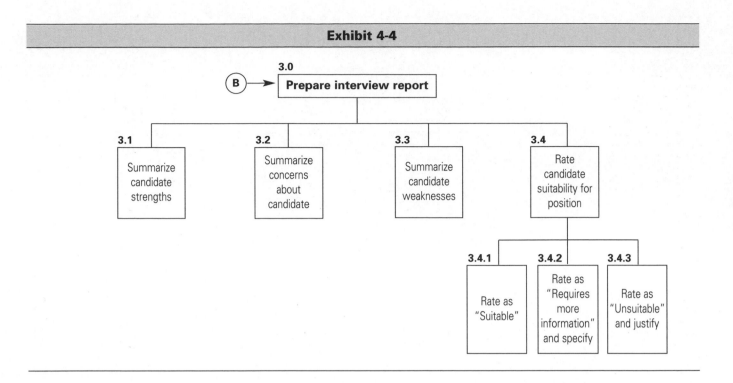

4. There are many task-analysis methods. The one we have presented here is called *hierarchical task analysis.* It works well in most cases to help break down the overall task into its simpler elements.

Here are some suggestions to follow as you conduct your task analyses:

- As much as possible, work with "real" experts.
- Starting at the top, ask your experts, "What does the learner have to be able to do to complete this task?" Think big. Force thinking to the highest level below the overall main task. In a hierarchy you are moving from the "monarch" to the "prince and princess" level, and then downward.
- The "thinking backward" approach to hierarchical task analysis is the toughest part of task analysis. It definitely gets better with practice.
- Continue breaking subtasks down. Stop each time you arrive at the entry level of the majority of your learners. Then move on to the next subtask until the task analysis is complete.
- The entry level of the learners is never stable. You will have to arbitrarily set what the level is, based on the majority of the learners. This means that, for some learners, you can eventually allow them to "test out" of simpler parts of the learning system. This can be a great savings in time and money for your training organization: You avoid unnecessary training. For less experienced learners, you may have to require prerequisite knowledge and experience. You may also create prerequisite learning materials and events that bring them up to the specified learning entry level.

During the hierarchical task-analysis process it is important to number each subtask so as not to lose track of it. The exhibits in the two case examples in this chapter show the numbering convention. When doing a task analysis, you do not have to work on a single board or sheet. It is easier to work on separate sheets, as shown in the second case example.

Spread out your work. Do not overcrowd your sheets. Later, you can list tasks and subtasks linearly, like this:

Conduct a Hiring Interview

1.0 Prepare for interview
    1.1 Prepare interview materials
        1.1.1 Review candidate's résumé
            1.1.1.1 Review educational background
            1.1.1.2 Review experience
            1.1.1.3 Review extracurricular content
        1.1.2 Review human resources assessment
            1.1.2.1 Identify strengths
            1.1.2.2 Identify concerns and weaknesses
        1.1.3 And so forth

An Activity for You

Task analysis is one of the most valuable skills you can acquire. It makes you truly learner- and performance-focused. It cuts out much of the content noise in training. It is the foundation on which you can

- create performance-based learning objectives
- develop learning checks and tests that verify the attainment of valid objectives
- design a module-based learning system
- build learning objects that you can reuse elsewhere for just-in-time learning or as job aids
- develop a learning and performance progress map
- transform the task analysis into a performance-management tool.

You should be sufficiently motivated at this point to conduct a task analysis yourself. Select a training program within your own area of expertise. State the overall performance outcome (for example, make a successful "solution" sale, operate a new software package, or interpret an X-ray). Break the task down into high-level performances (subtasks), as exemplified in the two cases we have provided. Derive increasingly lower-level prerequisite performances (sub-subtasks) until, for each task, you reach the entry level of the majority of your learners.

An Activity for Your Training Organization

Perform the same exercise you did yourself, but do it in teams. Conduct a show-and-tell to refine each team's task analysis. Ensure that subtasks contain verifiable verbs (that is, are performance-based).

Use the checklist presented in Worksheet 4-2 to verify your own and/or the teams' task analysis outputs.

Worksheet 4-2: Task-Analysis Checklist

	Yes	No
1. The overall task and all subtasks contain a verifiable verb. (You can measure and/or observe performance.)	☐	☐
2. At each level, all subtasks are necessary to perform the task or subtask immediately above.	☐	☐
3. At each level, all the subtasks added together are sufficient to completely perform the subtask immediately above.	☐	☐
4. If a subtask is broken down into lower-level subtasks, there are always at least two subtasks that break out of it. (If there is only one, you may not break down the subtask.)	☐	☐
5. All subtasks are correctly numbered in hierarchical format (1.0; 1.1; 1.1.1; 1.1.1.1; and so forth).	☐	☐
6. For any subtask, the task analysis stops at the entry level of the majority of the learners.	☐	☐

Chapter Summary

In this chapter you certainly went beyond the terms introduced in *Telling Ain't Training*—you went to their application.

- ◆ You reviewed some key training–learning terms and tied them all together. By doing this, you and your training organization have defined not only words, but also a philosophy that integrates training, instruction, and education into a cohesive whole.
- ◆ You have operationally defined the *Telling Ain't Training* mantra, "learner-centered . . . performance-based," and have developed a strategy for always maintaining a learner-centered focus.
- ◆ You have taken a powerful step toward being performance-based by engaging in task analysis. You have reviewed two cases, tried out the analysis for yourself, gotten your team members to try it, and verified your results.

So . . .

Now, the rubber hits the road. Go forth yourself and make your next training project a solid example of learner-centered...performance-based instruction. Conduct a task analysis. Share it with colleagues. Have them critique it and then model it themselves in their next assignments.

Following (or simultaneous with) these efforts, turn the page to the next chapter, which takes the human learner content of *Telling Ain't Training* and turns it into application for you and your training organization.

Chapter 5

The Human Learner

This chapter

- ◆ focuses on how to conduct learner analyses to make sure that you systematically get to know your learners prior to developing training for them.

Tools in this chapter include

- ◆ a guide to information gathering that indicates what information to collect on your learner population
- ◆ a learner-analysis protocol that offers guidelines for conducting interviews with sample learners
- ◆ sample learner-analysis interview questions that you can adapt for interviewing sample learners
- ◆ a template for synthesizing learner-analysis information, with a simple layout for reporting your findings.

The entire chapter 3 of *Telling Ain't Training* focuses on how learners perceive, process, and retain information. Our job as trainers, instructors, and educators is to design and structure what learners are required to master in ways that are most compatible with and relevant to them. To best mirror the learner's processing systems, to align ourselves with what helps learners learn, and to ensure that our instruction is designed in accordance with how learners best deal with incoming information, we must analyze our learners. This chapter of the *Beyond Telling Ain't Training Fieldbook* provides you with an assortment of guidelines and procedures for conducting learner analyses. Specifically, we offer you the following help:

- ◆ guidelines for specifying what types of learners you will be training and their volume (or throughput per year)
- ◆ procedures for conducting a learner analysis
- ◆ guidelines for selecting sample learners
- ◆ a tool that specifies what information to gather
- ◆ a learner-analysis protocol (guidelines for conducting learner-analysis interviews)

- ◆ a job aid with specific questions to ask when interviewing learners
- ◆ a template for synthesizing your learner analysis.

So, let's get right to work analyzing your learners.

Who and How Many?

Here are helpful guidelines for specifying what type of learners and what volume of learners you will train:

- ◆ Specify all of your target audiences. Notice the plural. Often, we receive a request for training (or generate a training initiative ourselves) that is focused on a single, specific audience (for example, sales representatives for Sales Force 12; customer service agents; installation technicians) as if that audience were completely homogeneous. Dig more deeply. Are we talking about novice or experienced workers? All levels of experience? Is what we will be developing only applicable to this specific group or can it (will it) be used with other groups (such as supervisors of the targeted group; part-time people who are also occasionally required to perform the same task; external, third-party partners)? Probe to identify *all* relevant learner groups and list these.
- ◆ For each group, note their job titles and any major characteristics that will significantly influence the way instruction will be received. Here are some examples of such characteristics:

  - • English is a second language for 90 percent of the learners.
  - • This is the first full-time job for 80 percent of the learners.
  - • All of the learners have performed similar work for at least five years.
  - • The learners are 100 percent on sales commission.
  - • All learners are former bus drivers who, because of medical conditions, can no longer drive buses and now are forced to perform clerical jobs until retirement (to obtain full pension). They feel they have been demoted.
  - • The learners are from the top 10 percent of prestigious university MBA programs.

  When you specify these major characteristics, you are signaling that they will have an important influence on learning.

- ◆ Specify volume or annual throughput. It is important to know the numbers because this can play an important role in how you choose to deliver the training and how much investment in training development is appropriate. The larger the audience (or annual throughput), the easier it is to amortize design, development, and production costs. For example, $100,000 spent to develop training spread over 1,000 trainees = $100 each. The same amount spread over 100 employees = $1,000 each. An investment as high as that latter figure may not be acceptable unless the return on investment is expected to be very significant.

- Note geographic dispersion of the learner groups. This, too, will influence how you deal with training delivery decisions. It may be more cost effective to send a trainer to four sites than to incur additional costs by creating Web-based learning.

Procedures for Conducting a Learner Analysis

The most common methods for conducting learner analyses are these:

- For each identified target audience, select a sample of learners (more on this to follow).
- Obtain permission from managers (and from unions, if appropriate) to observe, interview, and/or test the sample learners. By far, the most common technique for gathering information from learners is the structured interview. We provide an example of this a little later on in this chapter. Observation and performance testing can be very helpful in building a complete portrait of the learners, but these generally take large amounts of time and can be viewed as intimidating.
- Gather any existing data that are available about each learner group. Examples of existing data include
  - employment statistics (for example, years of experience, previous types of jobs, numbers of learners per geographic location)
  - educational background (for example, schooling, previous training, certifications)
  - work statistics (for example, performance results such as sales or average number of repair orders completed, ratio of exemplary performers to average and deficient performers)
  - types and volume of grievances
  - job descriptions or work expectations
  - overall or synthesis reports of performance appraisals
  - work climate study reports.

- Interview sample learners and take careful notes on responses. Watch out for biases you may bring to the interviews.
- Synthesize the learner-analysis data in a succinct, accurate report. We provide a report template later in this chapter.
- Use the findings of your learner analysis as key inputs to your training design. Respect who and what your learners are. Do not be overly influenced by what their managers tell you about them. Just because a manager used to be one of them does not mean she or he can speak for them. After all, weren't you once a teenager? Does this make you qualified to speak for your own teenage children or those of your neighbors?

Guidelines for Selecting Sample Learners

There are two main guidelines for selecting sample learners for your learner analysis:

1. Select, at random, typical learners. They should not be the best or the worst. Absolutely, positively, and *in no way* (is that strong enough?) accept the following as representing the learners you are targeting for your training:

   - managers or supervisors who volunteer to "tell you about the learners because I work with them every day"
   - instructors who offer to "tell you all about the learners because I teach them all the time"
   - the best, most experienced performers
   - those who have already taken the training (although these people may be helpful for reviewing your training when you have tried it out)
   - other instructional designers or trainers who will be happy to "speak from their experience with other groups"
   - even truly representative learners who volunteer to tell you about other learners (let learners speak only for themselves).

2. For each target audience you simply require a few learners, often not more than four to six. Here is why. If you adopt what is commonly called a *clinical approach,* you probe, in-depth, with each individual subject—listening, observing, and, if necessary, testing. You gain rapid insights about your learners. What our research shows in terms of quantity/usefulness of learner-analysis input is that after very few clinical instances, you obtain most of the required learner information for developing learner-centered training. Figure 5-1 shows what happens.

Figure 5-1: Quality and Usefulness of Learner Information Relative to the Number of Learners Consulted

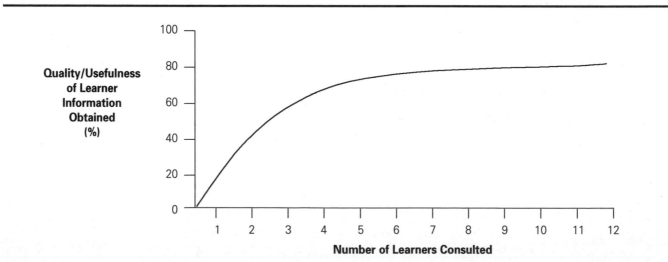

Determine how many different audiences you have (for example, novice/experienced/advanced; different job titles; different organization levels) and consult learners, one at a time, until you do not appear to be accumulating significantly new and different information from additional subjects.

A Template for Choosing What Information to Gather

The information you should collect during your learner analysis is listed below and presented in a template format in Worksheet 5-1.

1. Target population information:
   - primary populations, including job titles and organization levels, and key or major characteristics of each
   - secondary populations, including job titles and organization levels, and key or major characteristics of each.
2. Background and aptitude information:
   - current knowledge and skills in the task or subject-matter area
   - relevant background (for example, education, certifications) and experience
   - understanding of the learning/performance required
   - major misconceptions about the task or subject matter
   - specific and relevant background, experience, and/or aptitude deficiencies that might affect learning and/or performance.
3. Attitudes information:
   - general attitudes toward task or subject-matter content
   - subtasks or subtopics within the task or subject-matter content toward which there are very positive feelings
   - subtasks or subtopics within the task or subject-matter content toward which there are very negative feelings.
4. Learning method and language preferences information:
   - instructional methods and strategies that are seen to facilitate learning (preferences)
   - instructional methods and strategies that are seen to hinder learning (dislikes)
   - instructional media/delivery systems preferences
   - instructional media/delivery systems dislikes
   - language level and knowledge of specialized terminology
   - style of language preferences (technical, conversational, combined).
5. Tools and prerequisite skills information:
   - capabilities in relevant tools and prerequisite skills
   - deficiencies in relevant tools and prerequisite skills
   - other deficiencies that require special attention.
6. Other relevant information about the learners:
   - as a whole
   - as specific populations or subgroups.

Worksheet 5-1: Template for Learner-Analysis Report

Total learner-analysis sample size: _____

1. **Target Population Information**
   - Primary learner group
   - Secondary learner group

2. **Background and Aptitude Information**
   - Current knowledge and skills in the task or subject-matter area
   - Relevant background (for example, education, certifications) and experience
   - Major misconceptions about the task or subject matter

3. **Attitudes Information**
   - General attitudes toward the task or subject-matter content
   - Subtasks or subtopics within the task or subject-matter content toward which there are very positive feelings
   - Subtasks or subtopics within the task or subject-matter content toward which there are negative feelings
   - General comment: _____

4. **Learning Method and Language Preferences Information**
   - Instructional methods and strategies that are seen to facilitate learning (preferences)
   - Instructional methods and strategies that are seen to hinder learning (dislikes)
   - Instructional media/delivery systems preferences
   - Instructional media/delivery systems dislikes
   - Language level and specialized terminology knowledge
   - Style of language preferences (technical, conversational, combined)

5. **Tool and Prerequisite Skills Information**
   - Relevant tool and prerequisite skill capabilities
   - Relevant tool and prerequisite skill deficiencies
   - Other deficiencies that require special attention

6. **Other Relevant Information About the Learners**
   - As a whole
   - Specific populations or subgroups
   - General conclusion: _____

As pointed out earlier, you can gather some of this information from existing records or documentation. For the rest, the best approach is to go directly to the learners to collect what you require. In descending order, our preferred means for gathering the data are these:

1. face-to-face interviewing, observing, and, as required, testing
2. telephone interviewing
3. email interviewing with follow-up probing.

Time constraints and geographic distribution of learners often influence your selection of data-gathering method.

Specific Questions to Ask

Each learning/training project is unique. Therefore, questions will vary. However, there is a definite pattern, particularly in face-to-face or telephone interviewing. With email, because learners have to respond in writing, you must usually be more succinct. One way to get around this is via *matrix sampling.* You increase the number of sample learners, but ask each learner only some of the questions. Thus, if you have 20 questions and had decided to interview five learners, increase the number of learners to 10, but send each of them only 10 questions. You achieve the same result, but each learner has only half the number of questions to answer in writing. This increases both speed and rate of response.

As to what specific questions to include in a learner-analysis interview and how to go about doing this, we provide you with a learner-analysis protocol (that is, how you set up and run the interview; Worksheet 5-2, page 38) and a sample set of interview questions (Worksheet 5-3, page 39). The latter is *only* a sample. You will always have to make adaptations, depending on the nature of the project and your learners.

Synthesizing Your Learner-Analysis Information

Exhibit 5-1 (page 40) follows directly from Worksheet 5-1. It is the information-gathering template, filled in with sample information for a training program at Lightning Electronics. When you complete a template, filling in the requested information, you synthesize the data you have gathered and create a succinct report that describes your learners. Use this template each time you conduct a learner analysis.

An Activity for You

You have been presented with a broad range of tools, guidelines, and procedures for analyzing your learners. Being learner-centered requires this of you. Let's put your learner analysis to work. Select a learning project—something that requires you to train a significant number of learners. Using the materials and tools we have supplied, conduct a learner analysis. Use the results as key training design and delivery inputs.

An Activity for Your Training Organization

Introduce your colleagues to the concepts of learner analysis and the variety of tools and examples provided in this chapter. Have every one of your training developers conduct learner analyses for their projects. Review the results together as a team to verify what was discovered about the learners. Encourage the training developers to help one another. There is a huge payoff in this. Emphasize the value of tailoring training to learners' characteristics.

Worksheet 5-2: Learner-Analysis Protocol

1. Obtain client or manager permission to conduct the learner-analysis sessions. If unions are involved, obtain their buy-in and, if possible, their active support.

2. With the client, manager, or a delegated person, obtain specific learner names and contact information. Request 25 percent more names than you wish to contact because you will generally lose some potential learners as a result of other engagements or absences. Ensure that these people are all real and representative learners.

3. Contact (or have the appropriate person contact) each sample learner to set up your session. Here is an email example for an initial contact:

   Dear _____,

   We are developing a new training program/course on _____ that will be offered to people doing the same or similar work as you. I would very much like to meet with you face-to-face/ by telephone to gather your input. By working with you and others like you, we are more confident of creating the type of training that is most relevant to you and is designed according to the way you learn best. I can meet with you on the following dates: _____, _____, or _____.

   Please let me know immediately what is most convenient for you. The meeting will last no more than ____ minutes. Anything you share with me will be held in strict confidence. I look forward to learning from you.

   You can easily modify this message for a telephone call.

4. Set the meeting date and time. Confirm it in writing. If the date is more than a few days out, send a reminder notice or call.

5. At the actual interview session, use the agenda below or make suitable modifications. Go over each item with the learner before you start. Do this briskly, but in a warm, relaxed way.

Agenda

1. Introductions: interviewer/interviewing team and interviewee

2. Explanation of the purpose of the interview:

   - Desired outcome
   - Your input helps create a learning program/course that is designed to fit your characteristics, is interesting and relevant to you, and facilitates your learning.

3. Explanation of interview procedure:

   - Interviewer asks questions.
   - You respond freely—no constraints (except time).
   - Interviewer probes where necessary to obtain clarification.
   - Interviewer takes notes.

4. Basic rules:

   - All reports are anonymous. Confidentiality is guaranteed.
   - You may ask questions, too.
   - You can come back to a previous question and have the answer changed or deleted, even after the session is over. Here is the interviewer's email address/phone number: _____.
   - This meeting will last no more than _____ minutes.

Worksheet 5-3: Learner-Analysis Interview Sample Questions

Basic Information

- How long have you been with the company?
- What is your current job title?
- How long have you been doing this job in the company? In your work career?

Understanding of Need

- We have been asked to develop a training program to help you do _____. In your opinion, why should you go through training to do this?
- What do you imagine that the company expects you to do differently as a result of this training?
- Is this expectation feasible and/or reasonable in your view? Why or why not?

Background and Aptitudes

- Have you ever done _____ or something similar to it?
- With what results?
- With what problems?
- How did you learn how to do it?
- Was there any training? If so, what part of the training helped most? What part helped least?
- Was there anything that interfered with your learning? What? How?
- Do you feel you now can perform this task for which we are developing training? How can you demonstrate this?
- What would help you to get ready?

Attitudes

- What do you know about _____? Give me some specifics.
- If you learn how to do _____, how will it affect your job for the better? For the worse?
- Is there any part of this toward which you feel very positive? Very negative?

Learning Method and Language Preferences

- If you were designing a training program to help you learn _____, what would that program be like?
- Let's forget about _____. Think of a great course you have taken on any subject (for example, a company course; a night school class; a self-study course). What made it great?
- Now think of a terrible class or course you have taken. What made it so bad?
- Have you ever used any self-study materials to acquire new knowledge or skills? One for which you had no instructor? Was it an online course? On a CD-ROM? A paper-and-pencil text?
- How was your learning experience with that course? Good? Why? Bad? Why?

Tool and Prerequisite Skills

- There are some things you should know well or be able to do in order to _____. I'm going to list them. In each case, tell me if your knowledge or skill is strong, moderate, novice-level, or nonexistent. (Repeat for each knowledge or skill requirement.)

Other Relevant Information

- Let's leave the actual learning program aside. What do you think might help you prepare for mastering _____ before any training starts?
- What about materials that are clear, simple, and sent to you in advance to help you get ready to take the actual training? What is the probability that you would seriously review them? What would be the right amount of time that you would agree to spend on this "pre-work"?
- When you have completed the training, what will help you apply on the job what you have learned in the training?
- Is there any other relevant information you would like to share?
- Are there any questions you would like to ask?

Thank you for your help. If we are to design a learning program that will be useful to you, we need to know what helps you learn and what interferes with your learning. You've been terrific! Thanks again.

Exhibit 5-1: Sample Learner-Analysis Report: Lightning Electronics High-End Printers Program

Total learner-analysis sample size: 10 sales consultants selected at random during store visits, two per store from three stores in three states (California, Arizona, and Nevada) and two per store from two stores in Idaho. Experienced sales consultants (2+ years) = 4; novice/average sales consultants (6 months to 1+ years) = 4; part-time sales consultants (who work in a variety of departments, depending on needs) = 2.

1. **Target Population Information**
   - Primary learner group:
     — Computer hardware sales consultants:
       - approximately 40 percent have two or more years of experience
       - receive a base pay plus 1 percent commission, plus special incentives for certain types of sales
       - really like the incentives and commissions
       - are focused on volume sales
   - Secondary learner group:
     — Part-time sales consultants:
       - high turnover (70+ percent per year)
       - can be placed in any department, from cameras to televisions to computer hardware or software
       - receive low base pay plus 1 percent commission, plus incentives
       - mostly act as fill-ins for absent sales consultants during peak sales times (holidays, sales) or during low-volume, undesirable time slots

2. **Background and Aptitude Information**
   - Current knowledge and skills in the task or subject-matter area:
     — All sales consultants, experienced or new, have a general knowledge of their four printer brands and various models. Because printers generally are sold as part of a bundled package, consultants know just enough to describe key features.
     — Part-time sales consultants know very little about printers. They read information to the customers right off the product sheets. If questions become too technical, they find an experienced sales consultant to respond.
   - Relevant background (for example, education, certifications) and experience:
     — Mostly sales experience in consumer electronics. Most sales consultants have at least two years of college. Some have degrees. In general, knowledge of printer technologies, brand differentiation, and why some printers cost more than others is low. Experienced sales consultants and some new ones have taken short (two- to four-hour) courses on printer technologies.
     — They have virtually no understanding of the value of high-end printers ($500+) compared with cheaper ($99-$300) models to professional and small-business buyers. Experienced sales consultants can explain speed, volume, quality, and durability benefits. Most, however, focus on "sell them what they ask for."
   - Major misconceptions about the task or subject matter:
     — There is too much to learn, and printer technologies and models change too fast.
     — Cheaper printers work pretty much the same as higher-end ones, except for speed and perhaps quality.
     — All customers want is the lowest price to do the job.
     — Giving the customer what she or he asks for is excellent customer service. If you try to "up-sell," you can lose the customer.

3. **Attitudes Information**
   - General attitudes toward task or subject-matter content:
     — The specifications sheets are usually enough for helping the customer.
     — Go with the least-expensive solution package for the customer.
     — Printers are an add-on. The focus should be on the CPU and monitor.
     — There's too much information to learn, and it changes too fast.

- Subtasks or subtopics within the task or subject-matter content toward which there are very positive feelings:
  - Higher commissions for higher-end sales
  - Personal satisfaction of putting together a "professional package" for business customers (being seen as a knowledgeable professional)
  - Special effects and benefits of higher-end printers
  - New types of printer technologies (for example, laser color at lower price point, image manipulation in the printer, printer scanning options)
- Subtasks or subtopics within the task or subject-matter content toward which there are negative feelings:
  - Printer technology details are hard to learn and retain, and even worse to explain to most customers.
  - It is harder to sell a high-end printer than a cheaper one. It also takes more time and therefore is not worth it.
  - Pushing a high-end printer feels like you are selling something most customers are not asking for. It is high-pressure sales.
- General comment: Because of volume, consultants see themselves more as "transactional" sellers than as "consultative" sellers.

4. Learning Method and Language Preferences Information

- Instructional methods and strategies that are seen to facilitate learning (preferences):
  - Interactive demonstrations that focus on selling to customers
  - Hands-on practice
  - Realistic role play
  - Questions and answers
  - Quick-reference guides
- Instructional methods and strategies that are seen to hinder learning (dislikes):
  - Long, one-way lectures with PowerPoint slides
  - Detail on "feeds and speeds"—technology info dump
  - No connection with value to the customers and how to sell
  - Thick, technical manuals
  - Meaningless, memorization tests
- Instructional media/delivery systems preferences:
  - Live, interactive, short classes with real equipment
  - Learning software that is very visual/graphic and lets you simulate working with the printer
  - Quick-reference guides (pocket and online)
- Instructional media/delivery systems dislikes:
  - Boring live classes that are technical, info-dump lectures
  - Text-dense, self-study materials (online and print)
  - Thick, dense reference materials written by engineers
- Language level and specialized terminology knowledge:
  - Simple 9th- to 10th-grade English; basic printer vocabulary
  - Technical language level that can be used with average-consumer customers
- Style of language preferences (technical, conversational, combined):
  - Conversational languages, with stock phrases that can be used with customers
  - Technical terms, but not ones that require highly technical background

(continued on page 42)

Exhibit 5-1: Sample Learner-Analysis Report: Lightning Electronics High-End Printers Program (continued)

5. Tool and Prerequisite Skills Information

- Relevant tool and prerequisite skill capabilities:
  - Quickly hook up various printers to different CPUs
  - Run printer demonstrations
  - Clearly explain dpi, resolution, variability in ppm, differences in inkjet and laser jet technologies, cost per page, drum changes, and other basic aspects of printers
  - Explain value: price-performance-benefits
  - Basic selling skills
- Relevant tool and prerequisite skill deficiencies:
  - Consultative selling
  - Deep understanding of printer technologies and the cost value factors of various printer features
  - Knowledge of printing beyond the basics most customers know
- Other deficiencies that require special attention:
  - Nothing specific; but, in general, new and part-time sales consultants lack basic knowledge and sufficient confidence to adequately sell higher-end printers.

6. Other Relevant Information About the Learners

- As a whole:
  - Experienced sales consultants take it as a point of pride to know a fair amount about the products they sell. However, this does not appear to be a "store" value. Volume of sales overshadows everything.

- Specific populations or subgroups:
  - Part-time sales consultants (especially) are "at sea" with little support. They are glorified "go-fers" much of the time and often know less than the customers, which does little for the store's image and credibility.

- General conclusion: Overall background knowledge and skills to consistently and consultatively sell high-end printers is weak. The culture of the stores is also nonsupportive, despite words to the contrary. This will have a major impact on learners during and subsequent to training.

Chapter Summary

This chapter on the human learner has been an intensive one because being learner-centered is essential to meeting individual and organizational performance goals. Telling—transmitting a vast amount of information—simply does not work. It's a shameful waste. Look at the territory you have traversed in this chapter:

- You briefly revisited the main job of the trainer/instructor: to design and structure what it is that learners are required to master in ways that are most compatible with them. Therefore, you had to find out as much information as possible about your learners.
- You considered an array of guidelines, procedures, tools, and templates to get to know your learners better. You now possess a tool kit for systematically conducting learner analyses. You have seen examples of how this can be done.

◆ You have the rationale and an assignment to try out learner analysis yourself and to get your colleagues to engage in this highly rewarding and not-too-difficult activity.

So, here's the good news. If you do a proper learner analysis for a specific target audience, it is not necessary to redo it completely for additional training programs directed at the same audience. You only have to focus on the unique requirements generated by a new content or task.

What are you waiting for? It's time to press onward with learner analysis. Then, let's turn our attention to getting our learners to learn. This is the subject of the next chapter that awaits you.

Chapter 6

Getting Learners to Learn

This chapter

- ◆ reviews the differences between declarative and procedural knowledge—a rapid refresher
- ◆ has you selecting the right training methods to help your learners learn most efficiently
- ◆ helps you select interesting instructional strategies that bring your training methods to life
- ◆ reviews the key ingredients for learning from *Telling Ain't Training* and then helps you select remedial activities to compensate for deficiencies in your learners.

Tools in this chapter include

- ◆ a declarative or procedural objective worksheet—a decision table that helps you identify the type of knowledge a given objective requires
- ◆ an instructional methods selection worksheet—a tool based on a great deal of research into learning that helps you rapidly select the training methods to apply for mastering any learning objective
- ◆ a list and descriptions of instructional strategies—a table that presents you with a menu of instructional options
- ◆ a tool for selecting remedial actions to compensate for deficient ingredients affecting learning—a two-column table that offers actions you can take to help learners overcome deficiencies in ability, prior knowledge, or motivation.

One of the major training fallacies is the belief that someone who knows how to do something really well, an expert, is the best person to transfer this knowledge to those who do not possess it. Not only is this simply not true; it sets up a broad array of expectations that cannot be met. It also creates a counterproductive set of activities that defeat the purpose for which they were intended.

Imagine that you know very little about sound equipment but would love to purchase a great sound system for your home. You go to Lightning Electronics, a well-known consumer electronics store that has a specialized audio department. Your objective is this:

> *Based on my taste in music, home configuration, and budget, I'll select, purchase, and install the best sound system for me.*

You enter the store and meet Herman, the expert audio guy. You tell him what you want. He listens for a moment and then launches into a learned discourse about advances in audio technology and the benefits of a single 805 triode tube per channel. The one they currently have is rated at 21 wpc in class A and uses a 300B follower to drive the output stage. Herman says its dynamics are incredible, and he's eager to demonstrate this by playing a traditional Japanese drum track . . . .[1]

Well, you're awed by his knowledge and enthusiasm, but you can't wait to escape his grasp! He may have incredible "declarative" or talk-about knowledge, but his abilities to analyze your entry-level state and your needs and then help you attain your objective are not at all evident. In other words, he seems to have poor "procedural" knowledge—he doesn't know how to sell based on customer characteristics and needs.

This is a gigantic problem in workplace training. Management often takes the people who know a lot and sends them off to train others who know much less. Transforming declarative knowledge into procedural knowledge is very difficult. Most expertise is gained over time and through trial and error. Being able to do does not guarantee being able to structure the conditions that result in learners being able to perform. (Review pages 32 to 34 of *Telling Ain't Training* for a more complete explanation.)

Declarative Versus Procedural Knowledge: What's the Difference?

The bottom line: Declarative and procedural knowledge each employ different forms of processing in the human brain. *Knowing* how to do does not translate very easily (if at all) into *helping* people do. The reverse is equally true. Being able to name, explain, and describe does not necessarily result in the right actions. Here are some examples of this:

+ an "expert" driver-parent explaining to her daughter how to shift gears while learning to drive
+ an acclaimed basketball star coaching a losing team on how to score more points
+ a local citizen explaining to a tourist how to find a location (and, of course, "You just can't miss it")
+ a grandparent trying to explain how you make that delicious dish you have loved all of your life.

In all cases, they can do it (that is, they have procedural knowledge). But they may not be able to translate this expert capability into sound learner transformation.

Worksheet 6-1 helps you determine whether what the learners are supposed to be able to master is declarative knowledge or procedural knowledge. In the next section, Table 6-1 on page 52 helps you identify what it will take for a learner to acquire that knowledge.

Worksheet 6-1: Differentiating Declarative Objectives From Procedural Objectives

1. Define what your learner is supposed to be able to do as a result of your training. This derives from the performance-based task analysis. You define what has to be done as objectives.

2. Examine each objective. Apply the decision table below to determine whether attainment of it will result in declarative or procedural knowledge. There are a few cases where both types of knowledge are required. Identify these as well.

If the objective requires that learners . . .	Then the type of knowledge to be acquired is . . .
name, list, identify, define, differentiate between, match, point to, recall, select, state, explain, or in any way simply talk about something	declarative knowledge
do something, such as perform an operation, manipulate objects or symbols, build, create, perform a procedure, solve a problem, or apply knowledge to achieve a result	procedural knowledge

---

To verify that this is clear, apply Worksheet 6-1 to the following four objectives, which are drawn from the "Conduct a Hiring Interview" task analysis in chapter 4. Place a *D* beside the objective if it requires declarative knowledge or a *P* if procedural knowledge is needed.

_____   1.   Prepare the interview environment.
_____   2.   Describe the company and the available position.
_____   3.   Probe for clarification of interviewees' responses.
_____   4.   Clarify the next steps in the hiring process.

Objective 1. *Prepare the interview environment* has you setting up the table and chairs, adjusting the lighting, placing materials in accessible places, and making the atmosphere comfortable. This is procedural—*do*—knowledge.

Objective 2. *Describe the company and the available position* requires you to talk about two things in some detail. It is largely a recitation of facts from recall memory. Hence, declarative—*tell*—knowledge.

Objective 3. *Probe for clarification of interviewee's responses* has you analyzing what is said, identifying areas of ambiguity or indefiniteness, formulating probing questions, listening, directing, and more. Once again, procedural knowledge.

Objective 4. *Clarify the next steps in the hiring process* asks you to recite procedural steps. Talk about—therefore, declarative knowledge.

As simple as this seems, it is important because classifying what is required by the learner—that is, declarative or procedural knowledge (or both)—leads directly to identifying the type of learning required and the methods you apply to make that learning happen:

| Type of knowledge | → | Type of learning | → | Learning methods | → | Learning |

Helping Learners Learn: Choose the Right Methods

The good news is that there has been a great deal of research carried out on how we acquire both declarative knowledge and procedural knowledge. Declarative knowledge requires *memory* learning. Procedural knowledge requires *use* learning. Let's play this out using Worksheet 6-1.

1. Select an objective (for example, prepare the interview environment).
2. Determine whether the type of knowledge required is declarative or procedural. If it is declarative knowledge, the type of learning required involves memory. If procedural knowledge, the type of learning required involves use. (In our example, preparing the interview environment requires involves use, so it demands procedural knowledge.)
3. For memory learning, you have two choices: "recognize learning" or "recall learning." (The former merely requires you to identify something as known; the latter asks you to retrieve and recite information you have stored.) For use learning, you can apply concepts, principles, and procedures.[2] Look at the definitions below and select which class of learning your objective fits.

Category	Definition
Concept	Class or category of items, either concrete or abstract, that share a set of common characteristics (critical attributes), but may differ in other ways (variable attributes). *Square* is a concrete concept. *Customer service* is an abstract concept.
Principle	A cause–effect relationship or a truism that can be applied to a range of situations. *What goes up must come down* and *Goodness is its own reward* are principles.
Procedure	A set of steps that leads to a prespecified outcome. *Starting a car* and *calculating a person's credit rating* are procedures.

(In our example, preparing the interview environment requires the learner to apply various principles related to comfort, communication, and atmosphere.)

4. Design your instruction based on the "methods" listed for the category of learning that matches your objective. (In our example, preparing the interview environment falls into the "principle" category of learning, so you would state each principle, explain it, relate it to prior knowledge, and so forth, as shown in Figure 6-1.)

Figure 6-1: Instructional Methods Selection Schema

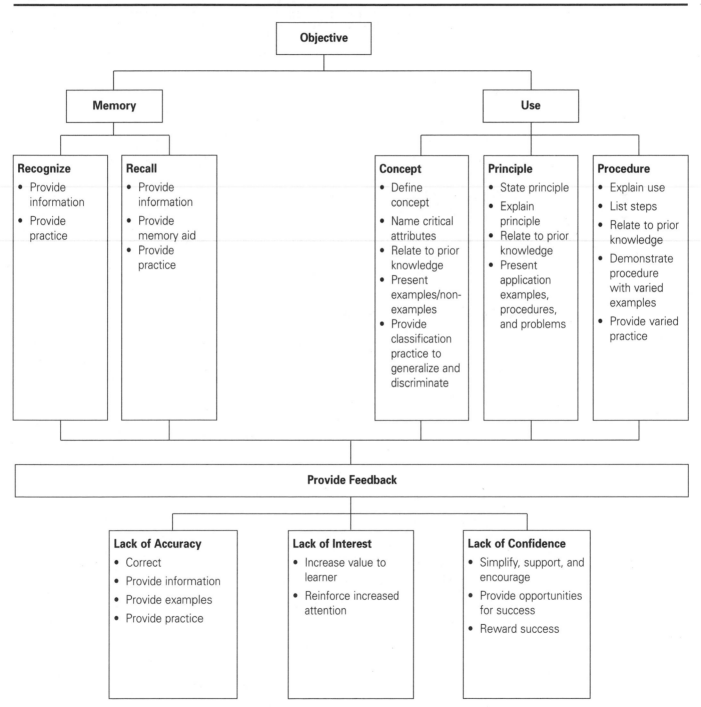

An Activity for You

Using either the task analysis you conducted earlier or the objectives from one of your existing training modules or courses, list the objectives (what the learner will be able to do as a result of the training). Examine each objective. Decide if it results in declarative or procedural knowledge (or in rare instances, in both types of knowledge). Determine the type of learning—declarative (memory); procedural (use)—and the appropriate category of learning for each (memory: recognize or recall; use: concept, principle, or procedure). Note the appropriate methods you should apply to help the learner master the objective. Follow those methods and create your training. You can bring these "dry" methods to life by embedding them in interesting, highly interactive instructional strategies. Table 6-1: Instructional Strategies gives you a useful starter list.[3] Remember, you can embed the methods recommended in Figure 6-1 into all of these instructional strategies.

Draw on these instructional strategies, making sure you apply the appropriate methods, as you develop training to meet at least one objective.

An Activity for Your Training Organization

Go back to pages 32 to 35 in *Telling Ain't Training* and review the differences between declarative and procedural knowledge. Emphasize the importance of these differences, using content from the early part of this chapter. Complete the same exercise described for you above. Debrief the results with your group as a whole.

The Key Ingredients for Learning

The three key ingredients are *ability, prior knowledge,* and *motivation.* Our major task is to compensate for whichever of these ingredients our learners lack. In overview,

- **Ability:** the capacity with which we were born that enables us to learn. Each of us has different types and amounts of ability, just as each of us possesses differing physical traits. There is overall general ability to learn, and specific abilities that determine how well we can learn to do specific things, such as sing, do math, or play a sport.
- **Prior knowledge:** how much we know about something before we try to learn more. The amount of (declarative and/or procedural) knowledge we have already acquired directly affects our learning something new. If you already know how to drive a Toyota, then learning to drive a Chevrolet will be easy for you; it will be harder for a nondriver.
- **Motivation:** the degree to which we are prepared to invest effort, resources, time, and even risk to learn something new. The more we value the new learning, feel confident yet meaningfully challenged, and are positive about it, the more motivated we are to learn.

Table 6-1: Instructional Strategies

Strategy	Description
Interactive lecture	Instructor presents information in a two-way (instructor ↔ learner) or multiple-way (instructor ↔ learners ↔ learners) communication. This strategy usually includes a great deal of question-and-answer interaction.
Hands-on laboratory	This is guided, hands-on learner practice of principles and procedures with feedback and/or exploration. This sometimes requires a special practice environment with appropriate equipment.
Reading	Learning from text in print or on screen. Can include tools, procedures, and guidelines to apply.
Interactive reading	Written material in the form of exercises, cases to solve, self-checklists and job aids to apply. This strategy often includes feedback about the learner's activity and results.
Self-study	Structured content that is based on the objectives and leads the learner (who interacts with the material on his or her own) to attain the objective. Each objective usually generates exercises, self-tests, and feedback. Self-study is sometimes referred to as *asynchronous learning* because it is not time-bound and in sync with an instructor's presence.
Simulation	The learner interacts with a concrete or abstract representation of a system (a real or imaginary one). To learn how the system works and how to master it, the learner manipulates or copes with system elements and events.
Game	This is an activity that challenges the learner-player, makes him or her follow certain rules and rewards, or punishes the player with points or lack of progress. There is always a "win rule" (or set of rules).
Simulation game	This is a learning design that combines the dynamic characteristics of simulation with the challenge of a game.
Peer learning	This is an activity in which learners learn from each other. Sometimes the activity is highly structured and the peer-tutor receives preparation and materials. However, peer learning can also be informal and involve mutual coaching and feedback.
Case study	This type of learning activity provides learners with scenarios based on real or hypothetical situations, and may include additional relevant documentation. Using the information provided in the case, the learner, alone or in a team, analyzes what is provided, and then tries to make sense of it, make appropriate decisions, and/or solve the case.
Behavior modeling	The instructor or a video offers a model of how things should be done. Learners rehearse and practice with feedback as cues are faded out.

(continued on page 52)

Table 6-1: Instructional Strategies (continued)

Strategy	Description
Role play	Learners are given (or create) scenarios, assume roles, and then spontaneously act out their roles as they try to learn about themselves and/or others—about how they act and feel.
Listening teams	Teams of learners listen to a lecture or observe a video. They take notes on a part of what is being said or done, and then share this with the group, sometimes in a different format. Often, listening teams are assigned the responsibility of ensuring that all other learners master their specific areas of listening responsibility.
Guided discussion	An instructor provides learners (teams or a whole group) with issues, challenges, and/or information, and guides logical discussion about these, eliciting facts, opinions, and concerns.

What can we do to compensate for our learners' ability, prior knowledge, and motivation deficits? Table 6-2: Remedial Actions to Compensate for Deficits in the Ingredients That Affect Learning helps you help your learners. It recalls Table 7-2 in *Telling Ain't Training*, but is now presented as a tool to guide you in adjusting for learner deficits in the three key ingredients for learning.

An Activity for You

Review the materials for a class that you have designed and/or delivered and that will be taught again in the near future. Review class evaluations, reports, and your own or the trainer's observations to identify what did not work. Determine if the reason for failure was a lack of one or more of the three ingredients. Whenever you note that one of the ingredients was a contributing factor, examine Table 6-2, select appropriate remedial actions, and adjust your training plan.

An Activity for Your Training Organization

Review the key ingredients for learning. Discuss in a group the extent to which "we" can and should do something to compensate for deficits. Also as a group, generate a list of specific ways in which everyone can adjust her or his training programs to accommodate for learner deficiencies. If feasible, examine one or two programs, pinpoint areas where learner difficulties have consistently occurred, and prescribe remedial actions.

Chapter Summary

In this chapter,

> ♦ you not only revisited and defined concretely declarative and procedural knowledge, but also developed clear distinctions between the two. You

Table 6-2: Remedial Actions to Compensate for Deficits in the Ingredients That Affect Learning

Deficient Ingredient	Remedial Action
Ability	• Break the learning into smaller chunks • Simplify • Use lots of concrete examples • Eliminate nonessential contents • Provide sufficient practice for each smaller chunk of learning to ensure mastery • Build slowly from the simple to the complex • Illustrate
Prior knowledge	• Create special learning sessions that focus on prerequisite skills and knowledge • Build connections with familiar past experience • Distribute materials that provide essential prerequisite information, with practice exercises as needed • Create tutorials and remedial sessions • Pair individuals who have prior knowledge gaps with those who can help them, those who can share their knowledge • Create study teams with mixed levels of knowledge, and make them responsible for helping each other
Motivation	• Demonstrate the value and benefits of the learning personally as well as to others • Show admired role models buying into the learning content • Build confidence by providing guided and supported practice • Include sufficient challenge to stimulate involvement • Provide success stories • Maintain an upbeat, positive atmosphere • Make learning fun and rewarding • Reward success

confronted the large problem created when experts are asked to train novices (so that the new learners can apply procedurally what they are taught). The SMEs, who have a great deal of procedural knowledge, erroneously try to convey that knowledge declaratively. What a mess!

- using a worksheet, you identified the type of knowledge required by an objective. Using a second worksheet, you linked the type of knowledge to the type of learning needed.

- you identified the methods that help build each type and category of learning (recognize, recall; concepts, principles, and procedures).

- you and your training organization received suggested assignments for putting the worksheets into action, adding instructional strategies into the equation.

♦ Finally, you revisited the three key ingredients that affect learning: ability, prior knowledge, and motivation. You received a table to guide you and your colleagues in overcoming learner deficiencies in each of these ingredients.

Now it's show time. *Learner-centered . . . performance-based* is your mantra. Take the time to apply each of the tools this chapter has provided. Your instruction will improve amazingly. Work with your colleagues to build learning based on solid, scientifically derived methods. Vary your instructional strategies while you incorporate appropriate methods into them. Remediate to compensate. Then, turn your attention to the next chapter on adult learning principles and their application.

Notes

1. Adapted from Silverline Audio 2005 International CES (www.silveraudio.com/index .php).

2. If you simply name and explain a concept, recite a principle, or state the steps in a procedure, this is memory learning, talk-about knowledge. Concepts, principles, and procedures are meant to be applied or used.

3. Mix and match these. For example, create a unit of learning to meet an objective that includes and integrates a game, peer learning, and guided discussion.

Chapter 7

Adult Learning Principles

This chapter

- ◆ opens with an examination of what constitutes "good" and "bad" classes, including how a good or bad characteristic affects learners
- ◆ reviews four key adult learning principles from *Telling Ain't Training*
- ◆ guides you in applying adult learning principles to a learning module or course of your choice.

Tools in this chapter include

- ◆ an adult learning principles worksheet—a simple worksheet that helps you generate ways to align a learning module or course with sound principles of adult learning.

An Activity for You

Here is a simple but revealing activity to open the subject of what works with adult learners. We begin with an exercise for you. Turn to pages 57 and 58, and follow the instructions in Exercise 7-1.

An Activity for Your Training Organization

Do Exercise 7-1 in a group. Create two common lists (good and bad). Discuss the effect of each characteristic on adult learners. Have them reflect on how each item might affect them personally. Then extend this to "our learners." Here are a few examples:

"Good" Characteristics	Impact on Me	Impact on My Learners
• It responded to my needs	• Kept my attention • I could see how I could use it • I worked harder at learning it • I felt I was gaining something worthwhile	• More attentive; less wandering attention • More participative • More enthusiasm and questions • Higher probability of using it on the job

"Good" Characteristics	Impact on Me	Impact on My Learners
• There was a lot of participation	• Kept me involved and awake • I did more • I remembered better	• Increased motivation and enthusiasm • More "lightbulbs" going on • They try things out and see the results first-hand
• I got feedback on how I did	• I understood better • I could improve • I felt great when I got it right	• Increased comprehension of what to do • Continuously improved in-class performance • Better preparation for application to the job • Less risk of error or confusion

"Bad" Characteristics	Impact on Me	Impact on My Learners
• I couldn't see how I would use it	• Boredom • Lack of interest to learn and apply • Frustration about wasting my time	• Lack of attention to what I'm training them on • Apathy on their part—nonresponsiveness • Impatience to leave
• The content was okay, but the methods for communicating were poor	• Frustration—I wanted to learn but got confused or overwhelmed • Hard to retain the content despite its value • Lost pieces of the content because my attention was split between following what the instructor was saying and trying to figure out what had already been presented	• Confusion • Loss of interest in the content • Erroneous learning • Eventually just turn off
• I contributed nothing or little to the session	• Felt like just another "empty vessel" into which content was being poured • I adopted a "just shut up and listen" attitude • The whole thing seemed impersonal and I lost enthusiasm	• Passivity, nonresponsiveness • No or little buy-in • No sense of being valued, which leads to eventual "turn off and tune out" • Sense of "why should I care?"

Adult Learning Principles Applied

In *Telling Ain't Training* (pages 46–60), we selected four key adult learning principles and demonstrated how, by adhering to them, you can greatly enhance the effectiveness of the training you provide. We quickly review these principles now, but if you need a more detailed refresher, turn to the pages noted above. Take a look at Table 7-1.

An Activity for You

Select a course that you have designed or are about to design or deliver. List the course objectives. Make each objective come alive by applying the four adult learning principles. By defining ways in which you can address each of the principles for every

Table 7-1: Four Key Adult Learning Principles

Principle	Explanation
Readiness	When adult learners see the ways they will benefit from what they are learning, they become more "ready" to learn. They open their minds to it. They are mentally and emotionally receptive to the learning.
Experience	Adult learners are not empty vessels. They learn best when the learning content and activities integrate with what they already know, and are readily assimilated.
Autonomy	Adults learn better when they participate actively in the training, and contribute to their own learning and that of other participants.
Action	Adult learners live in a constant state of conflicting priorities. If they see how they can credibly and profitably apply what they are learning immediately, their focus sharpens and their desire to learn increases.

objective, you will automatically become learner-centered. Use Worksheet 7-1 (page 59) to help in this task. To get started, turn to the sample worksheet completed for our ongoing example of conducting a hiring interview (Exhibit 7-1, page 60).

Exercise 7-1: Good Class, Bad Class

1. Think of a great class you once took. In the left-hand column below, list all of the characteristics that made it great. Be precise in identifying the characteristics. For example, don't merely list "instructor" but rather describe what the instructor did that made the class great.

2. Repeat the same activity, but for a rotten class. In the right-hand column below, note the characteristics that made it rotten.

Characteristics of a Good Class	Characteristics of a Bad Class

3. Examine the two lists and check off all of the characteristics or actions, both wonderful and rotten, that are present in most of the classes you create and/or deliver.

4. Review the lists below (taken from pages 44–45 of *Telling Ain't Training*). How do these characteristics compare with yours? Check off any items, good or bad, that fit with your training design and/or delivery.

(continued on page 58)

Exercise 7-1: Good Class, Bad Class (continued)

Characteristics of a Good Class	Characteristics of a Bad Class
☐ It responded to my needs.	☐ It was too far removed from my interests.
☐ I could see how it applied to me.	☐ I couldn't see how I would use it.
☐ There was a lot of participation.	☐ It was a one-way transmission of information.
☐ I was drawn in quickly.	☐ I soon was in information overload.
☐ The explanations were clear and concise.	☐ There was little to no discussion.
☐ I could relate to the examples.	☐ There was little to no practice.
☐ It applied to my job.	☐ There was little to no feedback to me personally on what I did.
☐ I could ask questions at any time.	☐ The materials were poorly designed.
☐ I didn't feel stupid.	☐ A lot of time was wasted.
☐ I understood where I was going.	☐ There was very little I could take back to my job.
☐ There were lots of takeaways I could use.	☐ The content was okay but the methods for communicating were poor.
☐ It helped me do my work better.	
☐ The session was interactive.	☐ I was a passive learner most of the time.
☐ I could try out what was taught.	☐ I couldn't understand what was being taught.
☐ I got feedback on how I did.	☐ The language and/or jargon lost me.
☐ There was warmth and humor.	☐ There were very few, if any, examples that I understood.
☐ I learned a lot from the other participants.	
☐ The materials were clear and useful.	☐ It was dull, monotonous, and boring.
☐ I felt respected.	☐ There was little or no class interaction with other participants.
☐ There was lots of two-way communication.	
☐ There wasn't a lot of time wasted.	☐ I was just another body in the course.
☐ The instructor "spoke my language."	☐ I contributed nothing or little to the session.
☐ I felt I added value to the session.	☐ I didn't learn much.
☐ I learned a lot of useful stuff . . . for me.	☐ I couldn't ask questions when I wanted.

5. Focusing particularly on the "bad" characteristics that are present in your training, use these lists to modify both the design and the delivery of your learning sessions. Include more of the "good" characteristics whenever possible.

An Activity for Your Training Organization

Divide your training organization team into peer-pairs. Select a module or course for them to review (a different one for each pair). After discussing the four adult learning principles and their value, have each peer-pair review its assigned course or module to determine whether adult learning principles have been applied and, if so, which specific one(s). Have them note strengths and omissions. Request that each pair make recommendations for increasing the application of adult learning

Worksheet 7-1: Applying the Principles of Adult Learning to Course Objectives

Course/Module Title: _____

Objective	Readiness (open their minds; show benefits)	Experience (integrate new learning with prior knowledge and history)	Autonomy (have learners participate and contribute to learning)	Action (show and encourage immediate application of learning)

Exhibit 7-1: Sample—Applying the Principles of Adult Learning to the Task of Conducting a Hiring Interview

Course/Module Title: _____

Objective	Readiness *(open their minds; show benefits)*	Experience *(integrate new learning with prior knowledge and history)*	Autonomy *(have learners participate and contribute to learning)*	Action *(show and encourage immediate application of learning)*
1. Given an interview candidate, prepare all materials required for conducting a successful hiring interview.	• Show two scenarios: unprepared for an interview and prepared for an interview. • Discuss personal benefits of complete preparation: professional image; better hire; fewer follow-up interviews; less wasted time spent in interviews.	• Draw from participants' personal positive and negative experiences as interviewees and interviewers. • Draw from participants their experiences or known instances of poorly prepared interviews and their consequences. • List what materials participants feel should be prepared beforehand. • Compare participant and instructor lists.	• Have participants share positive and negative experiences with interviews that were well and poorly prepared. • Draw from participants what materials they think are necessary. • Have participants review and discuss a job aid for materials preparation.	• Reveal the company hiring program and the participants' role(s) in it. • Point out how soon they will begin interviewing. • Discuss how their contribution to hiring will be tracked for their performance appraisals, starting this quarter.
2. Given a scheduled interview, prepare the interview environment to meet time/schedule constraints and physical and psychological requirements.	• Demonstrate the impact of a poorly prepared environment on the interview process. • Demonstrate the reverse—a well-prepared environment.	• Draw from the participants their personal examples of well and poorly prepared interview environments and the consequences.	• Draw from the group suggestions for preparing the interview environment in terms of time, room scheduling, and room/facility organization. • Have participants review environment preparation checklist and then practice with classroom furniture.	• Provide sample room arrangements and job aids. Point out that they will be observed and receive feedback on their first interviews. • Remind participants of interview schedule.

principles. Have them classify each recommendation as relating to the readiness, experience, autonomy, or action principle. It is acceptable for a recommendation to fit more than one of the principles. Debrief as a group, listing common inadequacies and how to overcome them.

Chapter Summary

In this chapter

- you adopted a critical point of view about the classes you personally and your training organization in general provide to your learners.
- you listed the characteristics of good and bad classes from your own experience.
- you identified which of these characteristics, both good and bad, were likely to be found in the classes you design and/or deliver.
- you added other characteristics from the lists we provided and then identified what you could do to eliminate the "bad" items and increase the "good" ones.
- you repeated the exercise with your group, adding two more dimensions: how your colleagues are affected by both the good and bad, and what the likely effect is on their learners
- you reviewed the four key adult learning principles, and then applied them to one of your courses
- you involved all of your training organization's instructional developers and trainers in a peer-pair exercise to examine existing courses and/or modules for application of adult learning principles. Based on findings, a debriefing elicited recommendations for increasing your application of adult learning principles.

This has been a brief chapter, but it has been filled with activities that can help you strengthen the learning effectiveness of your training efforts. We recommend that you and your team commit to consistently developing learning sessions based on sound adult learning principles. Review all of your training offerings and adjust them to be more learner-centered . . . especially *adult*-learner–centered.

To help you in this venture, the next chapter drives to the heart of *Telling Ain't Training* and the learner-centered . . . performance-based mantra. It focuses on a five-step model for building extraordinary training events of any length, both formal and informal. Forward. . . .

Chapter 8

A Five-Step Model for Creating Terrific Training Sessions

This chapter

- reviews the basics of the five-step model, which is at the heart of *Telling Ain't Training*
- provides an example of how to apply the five-step model and the training planning sheets that derive from this model
- guides you in "scripting" a lesson if it is to be conserved and reused by yourself and/or others.

Tools in this chapter include

- a training planning sheet—a one-page tool that allows you to plan a learner-centered, performance-based training session
- a training session scripting sheet—a template for building a training session that can be reused by yourself or others
- a training session planning sheet assessment—a checklist to verify that your training session contains all the ingredients that make for sound instruction.

The research literature on how to structure various types of learning is replete with models that explain and describe the what, why, and how of learning design. Sometimes these models are contradictory (that is, process-centered versus outcome-centered; objectivist versus constructivist). Often they are narrowly and specifically focused on one aspect of learning (for example, concept acquisition, creative problem solving). For training practitioners and workplace professionals seeking means to help workers learn and perform in valued ways, the plethora of models and their nuances can be confusing. How to cut through it all? There's the challenge . . . and what follows is the response.

Let's begin with a summary of what we presented in chapter 6 of *Telling Ain't Training*. There may be an enormous amount of scientific information available on learning, but what appears to have stood the tests of experimentation and time are these six key points:

1. **Why:** If adult learners know why, in a personally meaningful way, they should learn something—and they value it—the probabilities of their learning increase.
2. **What:** If adult learners know in specific but not confusing terms exactly what they are supposed to learn, the probabilities of learning increase.
3. **Structure:** If what adult learners have to learn is clearly organized and presented so that it is logical and comprehensible, the probabilities of learning success rise.
4. **Response:** If adult learners have sufficient opportunity to interact in meaningful ways with what is to be learned (that is, if they are mentally engaged in the learning and actively respond during instruction), learning success probability increases. The more the learner does that is meaningful, the more the learner learns.
5. **Feedback:** If adult learners receive timely (not necessarily immediate) and specific (but not overly detailed or confusing) feedback on their responses during learning, the probability of learning increases. Corrective feedback with respect to the task being performed improves performance. Confirming feedback maintains and strengthens what has been learned.
6. **Reward:** If the adult learners obtain some form of reward for learning, this boosts the probability of increased retention and application. The more the learner values what she or he is learning, the more the reward is intrinsic (that is, valued in and for itself). The less the learner values what must be learned (for example, transform a service call to a sales opportunity), the more extrinsic or external rewards play a role.

There is a great deal more to learning, but these six "universals" are extremely powerful and can carry you a long way. Figure 8-1 illustrates how we transformed them into something that can help you structure effective training sessions of any length for any population, on any topic, and for groups of any size.

Turn to pages 73–77 of *Telling Ain't Training* to review how you can use the Training Session Planning Sheet to create an initial design for learning. We have reproduced the example from *Telling Ain't Training* to demonstrate how the planning sheet works. Examine this example carefully. Start with the scenario that provides the background on the learning project.

Sample Planning Scenario: A Ticket to the Fair

Background: Once a year the state holds a large-scale fair. For one whole week, hundreds of thousands of paying visitors flock to it. Each year, the State Fair Commission hires temporary workers for various jobs. You are responsible for training 45 ticket sellers. They have to be accurate and fast because lines can get long and paying visitors may grow impatient. Accuracy and speed are the two key success criteria. The system is totally manual. All of the potential ticket sellers are novices, all have gone through background checks, and all are bonded.

Figure 8-1: From the Six Universals of Research to a Training Session Planning Sheet

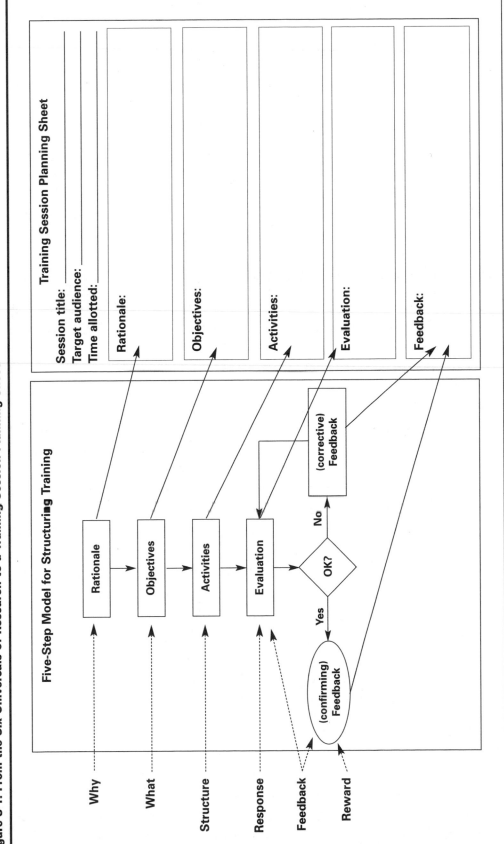

Target audience: Part-time ticket sellers with education levels ranging from grade 10 to some college. All are over 18; some as old as 60. About two thirds are women. None have dexterity problems or significant hearing or vision impairments.

Session subject: Calculating admission costs, taking money, issuing tickets, and giving change.

Time allotment: Two hours, 30 minutes

Training context: Classroom and crudely simulated ticket booths.

Now, review Exhibit 8-1: Sample Training Session Planning Sheet to discover how it forces a learner-centered . . . performance-based type of design. As this example illustrates, the learner is the central focus throughout. Equally, learners are engaged in "doing" right from the start and must demonstrate that they can perform as required by the objectives.

The Training Session Scripting Sheet

Taking our selling tickets at the fair example a step further, we can convert the plan into a "script" that an instructor can use repeatedly or that can be shared with several instructors. Examine Exhibit 8-2, on page 68, to see how the sample plan has evolved into a well-developed lesson or instructor guide.

An Activity for You

You are at an important—even crucial—point in the entire process. It is time for you to apply the five-step model, using the Training Session Planning Sheet to develop a unit of instruction. Select either something new (from your task analysis, for example) to create your design or rework an existing training module that is mostly content-centered rather than learner-centered. Be disciplined and rigorous in bringing to life the six universals of learning research, the five-step model, and the four adult learning principles you worked with earlier. We provide you with a blank Planning Sheet to work on (Worksheet 8-1, page 69). We are also offering you (from *Telling Ain't Training*) a Training Session Planning Sheet Assessment (Worksheet 8-2, page 70) to help verify whether you have met the learner-centered . . . performance-based goal.

Next, take a stab at scripting at least a piece of your instruction. Exhibit 8-3, on page 70, provides prompting directions for completing a scripting sheet. Worksheet 8-3, on page 71, is the actual Training Session Scripting Sheet for you to work on. Use the instructions in Exhibit 8-3 to help you.

An Activity for Your Training Organization

The worksheets and tools included in this chapter work just as well for retrofitting existing training programs to the five-step model as they do for creating new learning units, modules, and courses. Encourage your colleagues to apply the five-step model, the Training Session Planning Sheet, and, if applicable, the Training Session Scripting Sheet(s) in their efforts. Have them perform peer reviews of each other's work, using the assessment in Worksheet 8-2.

Exhibit 8-1: Sample Training Session Planning Sheet

Training Session Planning Sheet

Session title: Selling tickets, collecting money, and giving change

Target audience: State fair ticket sellers (15 participants per session)

Time allotted: Two hours, 30 minutes

Rationale:

- The most important and trickiest part of the job is selling tickets and making correct change.
- Despite background noise, if you've got the knack, you won't have problems.
- You are responsible for your errors up to $100. Learn the job right and you will be error free.
- Every day we have a bonus for the quickest and most accurate ticket seller.
- Some people get hostile when you are slow or make errors. This session will help you avoid the pain.

Objectives:

Overall objective:

Participants will be able to sell the exact number and type of tickets, collect the exact amount of money, and give the correct change for any customer without error and at an average time of 20 seconds per transaction (maximum group of eight people per transaction).

Specific objectives:

- Identify the exact numbers and types of admission tickets the customer requests.
- Calculate the exact total cost in 10 seconds with no errors.
- Collect the correct total amount with no errors.
- Give the customer the exact change with no errors.

Activities:

- Draw from participants what concerns them most about their new job.
- Show how this session helps decrease or eliminate those concerns.
- Present key points of rationale and discuss each one.
- Show ticket price/customer job aids and demonstrate use.
- Using different voices and admission requests, have participants determine exact request and cost. After several examples, time the exercise.
- Using play money and coins, have participants practice collecting money, issuing tickets, and giving change. This is a peer-pair activity.
- In simulated booths, create a practice session putting all parts together. Loudly play audiotape of background noise.

Evaluation:

- Practice exercises with timing toward the end for each activity.
- *Final evaluation:* In the simulated ticket booths, each learner serves 10 peer customers, each with different characteristics and requirements. An audiotape plays loud background noise. Peers talk. Trainer times each participant and verifies accuracy.

Feedback:

- Provide participants with feedback on how they are doing and how they can improve through self-assessment, peer assessment, and trainer verification.
- Provide timing and accuracy information following final evaluations. Suggest ways to improve, as necessary.
- Give prizes for best performance.

Exhibit 8-2: Sample Training Session Scripting Sheet

Training Session Planning Sheet

Session title: Selling tickets, collecting money, and giving change

Target audience: State fair ticket sellers (15 participants per session)

Time allotted: Two hours, 30 minutes

Objectives:

Overall objective:

Participants will be able to sell the exact number and type of tickets, collect the exact amount of money, and give the correct change for any customer without error and at an average time of 20 seconds per transaction (maximum group of eight people per transaction).

Specific objectives:

- Identify the exact numbers and types of admission tickets the customer requests.
- Calculate the exact total cost in 10 seconds with no errors.
- Collect the correct total amount with no errors.
- Give the customer the exact change with no errors.

Do	Say	Resources	Time
• Smile warmly. Pose questions to group.	• Ask: "As you face this new job as ticket sellers, what concerns, even fears, do you have right now?"		• Eight minutes
• Write responses on flipchart (F/C).	• Ask: "As I point to each item you have given me, raise your hands if you feel this. I'll write down the numbers."	• F/C and marking pens	
• Point to each item on the F/C, count raised hands, and jot down number.	• State: "As you can see, quite a few of you share the same fears and concerns. Let me assure you that this is normal. Everyone is a bit scared of the unknown. What is great for you is that this session will lay a lot of those concerns and fears to rest. Let's see why."	• F/C and marking pens	
• Show key points from rationale.	• Explain how this session prepares the learners to serve the customers, despite all the noise and pressures. • Stress the benefits and fun the learners will derive from the practice exercises in this session, and note that they may win prizes.	• Prepared F/C sheet with session benefits for learners	

Do	Say	Resources	Time
• Show prepared F/C with objectives. • Read, explain, and discuss overall and specific objectives. Move briskly. If there are concerns, put these on a separate sheet for handling later.	• State: "Here are the objectives for this session. Let's read the overall one first and discuss it. Then I'll briefly explain each of the specific objectives you will achieve by the end of this session."	• Prepared F/C sheet with objectives	• Three minutes

Worksheet 8-1: Training Session Planning Sheet

Training Session Planning Sheet

Session title: _____

Target audience: _____

Time allotted: _____

Rationale:

Objectives:

Activities:

Evaluation:

Feedback:

Worksheet 8-2: Training Session Planning Sheet Assessment

Criterion	Yes	No
The rationale is presented in terms of the learners.	☐	☐
The learners participate and contribute in building the rationale.	☐	☐
The performance objectives are stated in terms of the learners.	☐	☐
The performance objectives are verifiable.	☐	☐
The performance objectives are appropriate to the learners and the content.	☐	☐
The activities are appropriate to the performance objectives (they lead the learners to attain the objectives).	☐	☐
The activities require learner participation at least 50 percent of the time.	☐	☐
Learners can participate and contribute during the activities.	☐	☐
Evaluation is appropriate to the performance objectives.	☐	☐
Feedback is appropriate.	☐	☐
The session can be conducted within the allotted time.	☐	☐

Exhibit 8-3: Contents of a Training Session Scripting Sheet

Training Session Planning Sheet

Session title: _Take from the training session planning sheet_

Target audience: _Take from the training session planning sheet_

Time allotted: _Take from the training session planning sheet_

Objectives:

Take from the training session planning sheet. If there is an overall objective, state it first. Then include the specific objectives.

Do	Say	Resources	Time
This resembles stage directions in a play. List in order what both trainer and learners actually do—what can be observed.	This is like the script of a play. You provide the trainer with actual words or speaking suggestions. If the trainer requires content help, detail content points. If the trainer requires instructional methods guidance, detail instructional messages he or she is to state.	This is like the prop specifications for a play. For each instructional activity or event, list the media or resource requirements.	This is like the timing and pacing for a play. For each instructional activity or event, list the exact time allotment.

Worksheet 8-3: Training Session Scripting Sheet

Session title: _____

Target audience: _____

Time allotted: _____

Objectives:

Do	Say	Resources	Time

Note: Continue on as many sheets as necessary. Simply create your own sheets with the *Do, Say, Resources,* and *Time* columns.

Chapter Summary

Although this chapter has been short, it is a critical one. The five-step model, with its worksheets and tools, is at the heart of *Telling Ain't Training*. If you faithfully apply the model and worksheets, learner-centered . . . performance-based training will result. In this chapter,

- you reviewed the six universals from learning research
- you saw how the universals morphed into the five-step model for structuring training, which then transformed itself into the Training Planning Sheet
- you reviewed the application of all of the above to a training plan for selling tickets, collecting money, and giving change at the fair, and then saw it converted into a scripted lesson
- you then tried out the five-step model, applying it to your own content
- you applied an assessment to verify your plan
- you may even have done some scripting
- finally, you had your teammates try everything out, using a piece of their own existing training with the five-step model, and then debriefed the results.

Now, with these tools in hand, you can begin reviewing and revising existing training. Use the five-step model process to make it "the way we do our work around here." Everyone's satisfaction level will rise. Learner results will also markedly improve.

When you have launched into this valuable initiative, you will surely want your learners not only to learn, but also to retain their learning so that they can apply it to the job. Get ready, then, for chapter 9, which focuses on helping learners remember what they have learned.

Getting Learners to Remember

This chapter

- reviews the main elements of "metacognitive skills"
- helps you provide metacognitive support to learners
- presents six major sets of cognitive strategies, with explanations and examples.

Tools in this chapter include

- a worksheet for providing metacognitive support to learners—this tool takes the form of a decision table that begins with identifying symptoms, establishing the type of problem, and recommending what you can do to support a learner
- a table on cognitive strategies—the table defines each type of strategy and provides at least three examples for each one.

They learned, but will they retain it? Even more important, when the time comes to use it, will they be able to retrieve what they learned and apply it correctly? It takes more than just raw ability to learn well. Brute strength alone is not enough to win a battle; strategy is necessary in both learning and war. This leads directly to the discussion of *metacognitive skills,* described in chapter 7 of *Telling Ain't Training,* because these higher-order thinking skills are to raw ability as martial arts are to physical strength. Let's review these metacognitive skills briefly by looking at how researcher Richard Clark has described them:

- **Planning:** When faced with a new learning task, being able to reason out what must be done to be successful. This includes creating a plan to accomplish the learning (for example, proper mindset, best time, best location, organization of needed resources, elimination of interferences) and ensuring that the optimal conditions exist for learning.
- **Selecting:** Sorting out from all the information provided those elements that are necessary for effective learning.

- **Connecting:** Rapidly, almost automatically, and fluidly, building links between the new learning and prior knowledge. Creating personally meaningful analogies, comparisons, and similarities with what is already well known.
- **Tuning:** Trying out the new information in various ways to sharpen understanding; bringing the new learning into increasing focus until it is clearly understood—with no fuzziness.
- **Monitoring:** Verifying and reverifying not only progress in understanding and learning, but also applicability—how, to what extent, with what required adaptations, and with what variable results; adjusting to apply to new circumstances beyond those taught.

As we pointed out, these metacognitive skills are independent of a person's raw ability. They are like martial arts in fighting—independent of the size and physical strength of the individual. Good learners have highly developed metacognitive skills. They have learned *how* to learn. This is not true for poor learners. If you are truly learner-centered and performance-based and are dedicated to transforming, not just transmitting, then you have to consider your learners' metacognitive skills . . . and weaknesses.

An Activity for You

Worksheet 9-1 provides a tool for you to use. It combines elements from *Telling Ain't Training*, Tables 7-1 and 7-2 (pages 90 and 92), and then goes a little farther than both of those tables. It is in the form of a decision job aid. It asks you to observe your learners as they learn. If you spot certain symptoms, the chart helps you identify the metacognitive area of weakness and then choose appropriate remedial action. The more closely you observe your learners and perceive their weaknesses, the better able you are to intervene, build learning success, and increase their probability of on-job success.

Remember, our job as trainers, instructors, or educators is to act as a compensation for what our learners lack. Worksheet 9-1 helps you help your learners. Take time to review it now.

An Activity for Your Training Organization

Review Worksheet 9-1 with the group of trainers in your organization. Emphasize that more important than the specifics it contains is a profound concern for our learners' success. Of course, no one expects you or your colleagues to become learning therapists. However, sensitivity toward learner deficits and attempts to increase comprehension and performance create their own rewards for learners and training professionals. Determine feasible ways, as a training organization, in which you can respond to metacognitive skill deficiencies.

Worksheet 9-1: Metacognitive Deficits—Symptoms and Ways to Help Learners Overcome Them

If you've provided clear instruction, but the learner . . .	Then this is probably a . . .	And you should . . .
• Doesn't appear to know what to do or how to start • Randomly tries various approaches without prior organization or a plan • Uses whatever comes to mind, and tries to muddle through	Planning deficit	• Inform the learner of what it will take to succeed. • Provide checklists of required materials and resources. • Provide guidelines for preparing to learn by creating the right physical and mental environment, and budgeting adequate learning time, including a suggested learning/study timetable. • Review with the learner how to plan for learning success. Answer questions. Monitor performance.
• Applies what has been used before, whether or not it worked then. or now fits the new learning challenge • Doesn't know where to focus • Sees everything as important • Appears to believe that everything has to be learned • Is soon overwhelmed by the flood of new information, and is drowned in the details • Makes inappropriate or trivial selections on which to focus attention	Selection deficit	• Indicate clearly what is important in your instruction and all related materials. • Tell the learner where to focus attention and energy. • Review important points with the learner. • Provide cues to help select focal points. These cues may include bold headings and subheadings, underlined words and terms, page inserts with boxed critical information, and reviews of important items. • Prepare the learner to listen/read and select key points. Provide information as the learner takes notes. Review and verify what he or she selects. Provide both confirming and corrective feedback. • Provide note-taking guides or blank figures and diagrams that cue and guide selection of priority information. • Create frequent exercises and tests that emphasize essential learning elements.
• Views the new content as a mess to be digested whole, and attempts to memorize it without links to known skills and knowledge • Isolates the new learning from previous experience, and does not make use of what has been mastered previously • Creates erroneous or false analogies or inappropriate comparisons	Connecting deficit	• Have the learner recall relevant prior knowledge and link new learning directly to it. • Use familiar or easy-to-relate-to examples that make novel or abstract concepts, processes, principles, and procedures concrete. • Include analogies, metaphors, and other types of comparisons that build bridges between known and unknown knowledge and skills. • Draw on the learner's background or observations to create connections between what he or she has seen or felt and what he or she is learning now.

(continued on page 76)

Worksheet 9-1: Metacognitive Deficits—Symptoms and Ways to Help Learners Overcome Them (continued)

If you've provided clear instruction, but the learner . . .	Then this is probably a . . .	And you should . . .
• Has a fuzzy understanding of the new learning, but cannot bring it into focus • Continues to add more information rather than test, adjust, or eliminate what does not fit • Cannot create a clear picture of the new knowledge and skills, thus making errors • Applies the new learning in an overgeneralized or undergeneralized way	Tuning deficit	• Provide practice, examples, and cases that require the learner to apply learning immediately. • Create practice that focuses on large, obvious differences from the familiar. Gradually include exercises and application activities that require increasing amounts of subtle discrimination and fine-tuning. • Vary practice activities that elicit different learning and problem-solving approaches. • Evaluate and provide confirming and corrective feedback frequently, through self-tests, checklists, or observation and live intervention.
• During learning, uses known strategies, whether they work or not • Does not seem to have a clear or defined sense of progress in learning • Applies more effort instead of taking a different learning tack • In practice, applies new learning in rigid fashion (by rote), forcing what has been learned to fit all cases • Practices with few or erroneous adaptations • Does not monitor impact or make necessary changes conceptually or operationally	Monitoring deficit	• Provide simulation experiences that demand application of new learning in realistic contexts. Vary the nature of the experiences. Increase levels of difficulty. • Have peers monitor and observe each other during learning application. Use observation instruments and checklists to record application. Have peer learners debrief each other. • Observe live or videotaped application on the job. Question and debrief the learner. • Place the learner in on-the-job learning/practice situations. Have the learner self-assess, using structured assessment tools. Have experienced workers observe application of learning and give structured feedback. • Question the learner about his or her learning. Ask where there are difficulties and jointly select different learning techniques.

Note: Not all items listed must be present or applied for a given deficit. Any or all of the symptoms are indicative of a specific type of deficit and any or all of the listed remedial actions may be appropriate.

Cognitive Strategies

From metacognition or thinking about thinking and general strategies to learn effectively, we turn to cognitive strategies: ways to enhance your training, complete with job aids and tools for helping learners retain information better and longer.

In *Telling Ain't Training* (pages 95–104) we presented you with six major types of cognitive strategies. These are summarized in Table 9-1, and we've added examples of each strategy. To illustrate several of the examples, we've added Exhibits 9-1 through 9-4 (pages 77–80).

Table 9-1: Cognitive Strategies

Type of Cognitive Strategy	Explanation	Examples
Clustering	Way of arranging or organizing information for easier perception, understanding, retention, and recall	• Teaching similar products or tools together in categories that are easy to remember • Organizing the names of a group of people in alphabetical order • Placing events in chronological sequence
Spatial	Visual displays of information in layouts that allow a large number of elements to be readily perceived, comprehended, retained, and recalled	• A matrix that organizes information into a visually simple display (see Exhibit 9-1) • A Venn diagram that shows how various independent elements interact and overlap (see Exhibit 9-2) • A flowchart that shows how a procedure works
Advance organizers	Organized, short information packets at the front of something to be learned that create an expectation, build a vision, or sensitize the learner to what to look for. They help the learner prepare for what is to come. Often they relate what the learner will encounter to prior knowledge.	• A brief introductory sentence or two at the beginning of a text that tells the learner where to focus (see Exhibit 9-3) • A set of questions that prime a learner on what to watch for prior to viewing a video (a video viewing guide) • A recap of key points from previous chapters in a manual that are directly linked to new material the learner will encounter in the current chapter
Image-rich comparisons	Analogies, similes, metaphors, and literal comparisons whose purpose it is to build a bridge between prior knowledge and new learning material	• Comparing the work of a private investigator (known) to troubleshooting a piece of equipment (new learning) • Showing how the keypad on a computer keyboard (new learning) works similarly to a hand-held calculator (known) • The desktop metaphor (known) we use and view on our computer screens to manipulate software applications and files (new, abstract learning)
Repetition	Activities that have the learner practice and rehearse content in organized ways until she or he can recall it automatically and rapidly (see Exhibit 9-4)	• A computer-based game for railway personnel working aboard trains that shows 160 different types of signals. The learner must act appropriately each time as the signals appear at faster rates. • Practice with flashcards to learn the multiplication tables • Highlight key points to retain in study material. Convert these to test questions. Constantly ask the questions and respond with the correct answers. In each round, retain all questions incorrectly answered and then start again. Repeat until you can answer all questions perfectly and without hesitation.
Memory aids	Groups of easy-to-remember letters, words, or images that help learners store and retrieve more complex material	• Acronyms: IRS, ABCs, NAFTA • Rhymes: "i" before "e" except after "c" or when sounded "a" as in neighbor or weigh but weird is just weird • Acrostics: Richard of York gave battle in vain (the order of the colors in the spectrum of a rainbow: red, orange, yellow, green, blue, indigo, violet)

Exhibit 9-1: Examples of Spatial Strategies—Simple Text and Matrix Presentations

Here are two ways of presenting the same information about personal accounts for a bank's customers. Below the two versions are three customer need statements. Which of these two versions—text or matrix—works better for you in identifying the appropriate account to meet each customer's need?

Text Version

Here are our bank's personal accounts with their key benefits and limitations. Please select the best personal account for each of the customers presented below.

- **Money Market:** A customer gets the highest interest from this account and over time will see savings grow the most rapidly. Customers must maintain a minimum balance of $2,500 at all times and may only issue three checks per month.

- **Regular Personal Savings:** This account provides the customer with interest and there are no maintenance fees. The minimum balance requirement is $1,000 at all times. This account does not permit issuance of any checks.

- **Savings and Checking:** This is a hybrid account. It provides some interest to the customer and allows unlimited check writing. However, the minimum balance at all times is $1,000. Interest yield is very low.

- **Personal Checking:** This account offers easy access to money, and the customer may write an unlimited number of free checks. Minimum balance requirement at all times is $100. There is a $4 monthly maintenance fee and there is no interest issued.

Matrix Version

Here are our bank's personal accounts with their key benefits and limitations.

Please select the best personal account for each of the customers presented below.

Account	Benefits	Limitations
Money Market	• High interest • Savings growth	• $2,500 minimum balance • 3 checks/ month
Regular Personal Savings	• Moderate interest • No maintenance fees	• $1,000 minimum balance • No checks
Savings and Checking	• Some interest • Unlimited free checks	• $1,000 minimum balance • Very low interest
Personal Checking	• Easy access to money • Unlimited free checks	• $100 minimum balance • $4/month fee • No interest

Three Sample Statements of Customer Needs

Sharyn: "I'd like to get some interest on my money, but I have to pay my rent, electricity bill, and credit card payment monthly out of the account. I always like to keep a few thousand dollars in the account for emergencies and investments."

Type of account you recommend: _____

Ravi: "I keep most of my savings in certificates of deposit. But I need an account where I can keep about $1,500 at all times and write checks. I'd like some interest, but I certainly don't want to pay for my checks."

Type of account you recommend: _____

Maria: "I just got my first job. I'm also just starting out on my own. I need a bank account to deposit my salary and that lets me write a lot of checks to pay my bills. I don't earn much and I don't have much money for savings right now."

Type of account you recommend: _____

The answers are Sharyn, Money Market; Ravi, Savings and Checking; Maria, Personal Checking.

Which version worked better for you? More than 90 percent of respondents select the Matrix Version.

Exhibit 9.2: Example of a Venn Diagram Illustrating a Spatial Cognitive Strategy

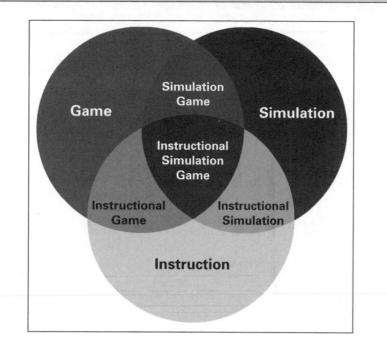

Notice how you can combine instruction with both simulations and games to create a variety of activities.

An Activity for You

For each of the six cognitive strategies there are application guidelines and suggestions in *Telling Ain't Training* and in Worksheet 9-1 here. Select one or more of the cognitive strategies and apply it/them to an item of content in a course you have designed and/or taught to increase comprehension, use, and recall. Try out what you create on a sample learner to see if it works. Adjust as necessary.

An Activity for Your Training Organization

As a group, review the six cognitive strategies, with examples drawn from *Telling Ain't Training* (pages 95–104) and this chapter. Review the uses of each strategy. Have each colleague practice one of the cognitive strategies, using his or her own content—either content already embedded in an existing course or something entirely new. Try out these strategies with the group and make revisions to improve the design. Share all of the outputs with everyone in your organization.

Chapter Summary

The purpose of this chapter was to help you help your learners remember. In the preceding pages,

- you reviewed metacognitive skills and their importance for learning
- you examined a tool—a form of decision job aid—that guides you in observing your learners, identifying their metacognitive deficits, and taking appropriate actions to help them overcome those deficits

Exhibit 9-3: Example of a Brief Introductory Paragraph to Illustrate the Advance Organizer Cognitive Strategy

You have probably heard that caffeinated drinks, especially coffee, are bad for you. Is this really true? In the report below, you will discover three health benefits that come from drinking coffee with caffeine. You will also find three potential dangers. List all of these in the table that follows the text of the report.

In the 1970s and 1980s, coffee developed a reputation for causing all sorts of ills, from high blood pressure and cancer to miscarriages. Drinking coffee just "seemed" wrong—a vice—so coffee had to be bad for you.

Today, researchers are finding that caffeinated coffee may have far more benefits than drawbacks for our health. Published studies in the last five years suggest a strongly protective effect of coffee against gallstone disease. In a Harvard School of Public Health study that followed more than 46,000 men, researchers found that those who drank one cup a day had a 13 percent lower risk of developing gallstones; two to three cups, a 21 percent lower risk; and four or more cups a day, a 33 percent lower risk. A 2002 study of 80,000 women came up with the same results.

In a 2000 Department of Veterans Affairs study of 8,000 men whose diets had been tracked for 30 years, researchers found that coffee drinkers significantly reduced the odds of developing Parkinson's disease. A 2001 Harvard School of Public Health study on men and women found similar results. And the more coffee consumed, the lower the risk.

The most far-reaching benefit of coffee appears to be in protecting against Type 2 Diabetes. *Lancet,* a British medical journal, published in 2002 a Dutch report that consumption of six or more cups of coffee per day decreased the likelihood of developing Type 2 Diabetes by 50 percent.

Amazing! But some concerns persist. Caffeine can aggravate heart arrhythmia. People who have trouble sleeping should avoid caffeine, especially late in the day. It increases insomnia. Finally, caffeine can find its way into breast milk of nursing mothers, negatively affecting their babies.

The bottom line: Caffeine poses no danger for most people. It may even benefit you. Cheers!

(Based on a special report to the *Los Angeles Times* by Peter Jaret, June 7, 2004, pages F-1 and F-4.)

Potential Health Benefits	Potential Health Risks
1.	1.
2.	2.
3.	3.

Did the boxed advance organizer at the top help you focus on and retain the three health benefits and three potential health hazards?

Exhibit 9-4: Example of How the Repetition Cognitive Strategy Supports Learning

Complete the two exercises below in less than 30 seconds. Time yourself.

Exercise 1

A B _ D _ F _ _ I _ K _ M _ _ _ _ Q R S _ U V _ X _ Z

Exercise 2

$8 \times 5 =$ ____ $4 \times 9 =$ ____ $7 \times 7 =$ ____ $3 \times 6 =$ ____

You probably completed both exercises in less than 30 seconds. The average time of our respondents is 15 seconds. Amazing! And why can you answer so rapidly and accurately? Because, through a great deal of repetition, the responses have become automatic, even if you do not have to sequence letters alphabetically all that often or multiply frequently. You see? Repetition works!

- you were encouraged to share Worksheet 9-1 with your group of training professionals and colleagues to determine feasible ways in which you as a training organization can respond to your learners' metacognitive deficits
- you examined six types of cognitive strategies to help learners learn faster and better
- you tried out one or more of the cognitive strategies with your own content
- you engaged your colleagues in activities applying the cognitive strategies

Metacognitive and cognitive strategies are extremely valuable in fostering effective, efficient learning that will be used on the job. Make it part of your culture to monitor and compensate for metacognitive skill deficits. The additional benefit is that you will help improve how your learners learn overall. Look for opportunities to package learning content more efficiently by applying cognitive strategies to the design of your training. Share successful examples.

You are now ready to take an active step forward to the next chapter. Active, because you will be encouraged to apply a number of activity-based training designs to meet your training goals. What are we waiting for?

Chapter 10

Training Approaches and a Cornucopia of Learning Activities

This chapter

- ◆ summarizes four main approaches to training presented as "architectures" in *Telling Ain't Training*
- ◆ guides you in determining which approach you should select for a given purpose and type of learner
- ◆ introduces games and game-like activities as highly effective training exercises
- ◆ provides guidelines, with examples, for rapidly creating learning games
- ◆ details a model for debriefing games, role plays, and other similar learning activities
- ◆ introduces the case study method, with guidelines for developing and using cases for training.

Tools In this chapter include

- ◆ a worksheet on the four approaches to training—a job aid that starts with clarifying the training purpose and identifying major learner characteristics to help you select the appropriate training approach
- ◆ a frame-game activity template—a format for detailing the important information about a game or game-like activity you design
- ◆ a D-FITGA debriefing worksheet—a planning worksheet that guides you in planning the systematic debriefing of an interactive activity
- ◆ a checklist of the essential elements of a "good" learning case.

There are many "approaches," "types," or "architectures" for training. The four that are most frequently described in the literature are *receptive, directive, guided discovery,* and *exploratory.* In her book, *Building Expertise,*[1] Ruth Clark presented and clearly explained these four approaches.

There are two reasons why these are of interest to you:

1. Learners with different types of characteristics and needs require different overall training approaches.
2. At various points in time, as learners become more expert in a particular area of knowledge or skill, they may require different training approaches.

Four Approaches to Training

In *Telling Ain't Training* we described each of the four approaches (pages 109–112). We'll briefly summarize their characteristics here and then send you on to a job aid, Worksheet 10-1, that matches learners with approaches. With this job aid you can select the most appropriate overall training approach for a given set of learners.

1. **Receptive training:** This is basically a "telling" mode. The learners tune in and receive what is transmitted. Learners become "aware" of new things. If done well, receptive training can build interest, stimulate motivation (by showing value and increasing confidence), and trigger a desire to learn more. If learners already have a strong background in what they are being taught, the new material may be enough for them to create new mental connections and be able to perform. This is a highly instructor-controlled training approach.

2. **Directive training:** As its name suggests, this is an approach to training that says to the learner, "Here is what you have to learn and here is the learning path to follow. Do what is asked and you will learn." This is, once again, an instructor-controlled type of training, but unlike the learners in receptive training, learners here do a great deal as they travel the well-laid-out path.

3. **Guided discovery:** We now move to shared control and responsibility for learning. The usual method here is to place learners into situations (for example, via cases, simulations, problems, events) and, with varying amounts of guidance, send them off to solve or resolve the issues and achieve some form of goal. Usually learners are provided with access to tools, materials, information, and support systems. They can get assistance if stuck. The central idea is to foster as much independence as possible.

4. **Exploratory learning:** In this approach, the training designer creates and/or organizes a resource-rich environment in which learners can explore and learn, based on their own goals. Learners control what they want to learn, how they go about learning it, and when they have achieved desired results. This approach blends beautifully with existing databases, knowledge-management systems, learning communities, and access to external resources. It is also possible to build small, self-contained learning environments that are designed to encourage specific forms of exploration for learning.

As you can readily see, the more knowledgeable and independent the learner is, the more she or he should be able to progress from receptive (rarely a desirable choice) to exploratory. However, there are times when a more directive and controlled approach is appropriate (for example, when learning how to escape from a burning building). Worksheet 10-1 on page 86 can help you choose the most suitable training approach for any given situation.

An Activity for You

Examine the training programs for which you are responsible. Review your learner analysis for each one. If you have not conducted learner analyses, you should initiate them. It is never too late. In the meantime, jot down major learner characteristics. Then, apply the four approaches to training as presented in Worksheet 10-1 to select the approach that best matches the learners and the program objectives. Take into consideration the dangers listed there.

The worksheet should help you determine the approach that best suits your purposes and the characteristics of your learners. Remember, you can always combine elements of each approach, but when you do so, be careful not to create confusion. Blend your approaches carefully.

An Activity for Your Training Organization

Develop a review plan for all of your training curricula. Have your group examine each curriculum and the associated courses over time. Using Worksheet 10-1, decide if the approach currently used is suitable for the learners. If not, or if there appears to be a more efficient and effective approach, decide on what would work best, taking into consideration potential dangers. Decide what must be done to alter the approach, if required. Emphasize as a caution that the group should avoid the receptive training mode as much as possible.

For you or your training organization, you can apply the four approaches to training matrix in Worksheet 10-1 at the curriculum, course, module, or even "learning object" levels. Just be careful how you combine these in training delivery.

A Plethora of Activities

In *Telling Ain't Training* (chapter 8, pages 115–136), there are 25 highly engaging activities that readily convert to a wide array of uses in your training. All of these have been tested over time and have demonstrated that they work with different types of learners and content. Table 8-2 in *Telling Ain't Training* (page 135) shows you what types of settings are most suited for each of the activities.

Now, let's take a step beyond what is there and add to your and your training organization's repertoire of interactive learning activities that vastly increase the probability of learner engagement and learning success.

Frame Games and Game-Like Activities

Just say, "Let's play a game" or "Let's break into a fun activity" and watch your learners suddenly become alert. There is so much you can do with games and game-like

Worksheet 10-1: When to Use Each Approach and What to Watch For

Purpose of the Course	Major Learner Characteristics	Appropriate Approach	Cautions
• Build awareness • Inform • Motivate	• Learner is self-motivated. • Learner has sufficient prior knowledge. • Telling is enough for transmitted information to stick.	Receptive training	• With no control, learners may feel like targets. • If the learner is not sufficiently self-motivated or doesn't perceive content to be important or relevant, he or she may tune out. • Very little sticks to the learner's brain. • There may be a mistaken belief that telling = training and that transmission = learning.
• Quickly build basic skills and knowledge • Create initial competence and confidence • Predict precise learning outcomes	• Learner is not necessarily self-motivated. • Learner possesses little prior knowledge. • Learner has weaknesses in metacognitive skills. • Learner lacks initiative or confidence to assume control. • Learner knows he or she will apply learned skills and knowledge in ways that are very similar to training.	Directive training	• May turn off more independent learners. • May imply one right way (or a narrow range) of doing things. • Does not encourage exploration or creativity. • Limits more advanced learners.
• Encourage learner initiative in a safe learning environment • Involve learners in case-based analysis and problem solving of increasingly realistic issues • Build wider transfer of learned skills and knowledge beyond what is taught • Build independence in learning while providing a safety net • Act as a next step in following directive training	• Learner has confidence to engage in discovery. • Learner possesses some prior knowledge about the content. • Learner has good metacognitive skills. • Learner is self-motivated to learn, but appreciates guidance and feedback.	Guided discovery	• For the less confident learner, there is possible stress or confusion. • For the independent learner, there is still too much outside control; the approach is too limiting. • Learner may require more time to learn than from receptive or directive training. • Outcomes are less predictable than with directive training.
• Create an environment for self-initiated learning • Provide maximum freedom for learner to take control of learning • Respond to a variety of learning needs that are highly individualized	• Learner is self-motivated to learn. • Learner possesses prior knowledge in content and/or self-initiated learning. • Learner has well-developed metacognitive skills. • Learner knows what is needed and knows how to find it.	Exploratory learning	• Learner can get lost. • Learner may waste time. • Not suited to a learner lacking the appropriate characteristics. • Learner may not learn what is necessary or may draw inappropriate conclusions. • There is little control and predictability of results.

activities to build learning and performance. (Incidentally, if your learners are uncomfortable with the term *game,* substitute *interactive activity* or *participative exercise* instead. Whichever word or euphemism you use, what follows works equally well.)

Uses of Games and Game-Like Activities

Games and similar activities are excellent learning vehicles for

- introducing new skills, concepts, or content. Imagine that your learners have never experienced outdoor winter activities in the snowy mountains. They are about to go off on a trip to such a region for work, but will have some time to enjoy outside recreational opportunities. A simple board game you have titled "Mountain High" has players follow trails where they land on "incident" and "question" squares, and either have to cope with the incident (or suffer realistic consequences) or answer questions about safety and survival. This game can open them up to the real dangers of what appears on the surface to be a winter wonderland. Similarly, a Bingo-like game that uses products instead of numbers can be employed to open a learning session for new hires at a home improvement megastore.

- integrating new learning by providing practice and feedback. Your learners are taking a boating navigation course and have learned about various cloud formations, their names, and appearance characteristics. Why not help solidify the learning with a Concentration-type game that has learners pairing pictures of clouds with their names? You could add humor to the title of the game by calling it "Bring in the Clouds."

- testing assumptions. How can we get an innovation to be adopted in an organization? Why not try to do this in teams? Using an activity called "Innov-Eight," various learner teams are given scenarios in which they have to figure out how to get an innovation (for example, transforming an instructor-centered, content-based way of training to a learner-centered, performance-based approach) adopted in eight weeks (derived from an adoption of innovation model). At each step, they make decisions and initiate actions based on information embedded in the game feedback.

- trying out strategies. In the 19th century the Prussian army played strategy games to determine the best way to invade and conquer Austria. Based on the strategies they tried out in their gaming sessions, the Prussians invaded Austria and within seven weeks conquered the country—a once-invincible power. Military, political, business, and economics strategists still use games and game-like activities to test their tactics.

- generating insights. Games and game-like activities can trigger "Ah-ha!" moments in learners. Sociologist Cathy Greenblatt created a group-based simulation–role play game called "Blood Money," which models how hemophiliacs have to deal with the medical system, family, and work. By playing the game, real family members, coworkers, and medical professionals see the world from the hemophiliac's perspective and achieve a number of valuable insights. A cross-cultural game-like activity called "Bafá-Bafá," created by Gary Shirts and used in military and corporate settings, opens players' eyes to how quickly they build up prejudices and readily make negative judgments about other cultures.

♦ evaluating learning and performance. You learned something; you can pass a written test. But can you apply what you learned? Why not see how well you perform in this game called "Confrontation"? You are a university-based pastor, often called on to mediate disputes. You have learned the principles of mediation, so "Confrontation" places before you a range of scenarios. The pastors form groups of three. Two of the pastor-players assume opposing roles in situations they might encounter in their work (for example, a female student who wants to marry and her mother who feels she is far too young). The third player is the mediator. They have a time limit to achieve consensus. Players rotate roles after each scenario. Everyone has tokens that are won or lost, depending on the degree of consensus in each scenario. The pressure is on to perform!

♦ building teams. Sivasailam Thiagarajan has created a wonderful game-like activity titled "Kindred Spirits." Virtually any number of learners can participate. A general topic such as "workplace equity" is given. Through a series of different rounds in which the activities change, naturally selected teams emerge that have like-minded ideas. They create a team logo, a philosophy, a T-shirt slogan, and an action plan. A variation of this activity, "Our School," has successfully engaged middle-schoolers in developing teams that come up with actions to improve the spirit of their school in very different but relevant ways.

♦ improving communication. Here's a game that focuses on building better communication on issues about which there are extreme views. It's called "The Great Debate." An issue that generates polarized positions is selected (for example, abortion, merit pay, plans for a megastore in the community, or government-supported universal health care). Participants take an opinion quiz (usually a Likert five- or seven-point scale type of test) that is easily scored and that establishes their views on the issue. Based on scores, the participants are divided into "for" and "against" teams. Those with neutral scores become the judges. To foster better communication, the "for" players are given a variety of subtopics on the issue. They break into smaller teams, each with one subtopic, and prepare to debate *against* the issue on their subtopic themes. Similarly, the "against" players prepare to debate *for* the issue. Assuming positions opposite to those they normally hold forces participants to consider the other point of view. Debate ensues (each team has two minutes). The judges decide the winning team, based solely on debating points. A general debriefing follows.

- revealing to participants how easy it is to mangle communication when it travels a distance from the source. Try the children's game called "Broken Telephone" or "The Whisper Game." A phrase is repeatedly whispered from one player to the next, until the last person repeats the phrase aloud (and likely discovers it's nothing like the original phrase).

- creating action plans. Several of the games and game-like activities mentioned above readily lend themselves to action planning. The "Mountain High" game can feed right into the creation of safety action plans. The same is true for "Innov-Eight," war and business games, and variations of "Kindred Spirits." There are, however, specific games and game-like structures that are designed to achieve action planning. One of these, "NAG (Needs Analysis Game)" by Thiagarajan takes any number of participants and, after separating them into teams, generates a prioritized list of needs with respect to an issue (for example, increase promotions for women and minorities, provide better service to elderly riders on our buses, penetrate new markets, or solution sell [as opposed to product sell]). The outcome of this highly involving activity is not only a priority list of needs, but also concrete actions participants will initiate and support. The power of this game-like design is that those charged with carrying out the actions are the ones who generated them. Buy-in is high.

And so much more. . . . These engaging games and game-like "designs" are all learner-centered and performance-based. Outcomes are verifiable and generated by the participant-learners themselves. Other potential uses of these designs include operational planning, problem solving, learning a foreign language, and discovering how a system works.

Why Do Games and Game-Like Activities Work?

The four main reasons are these:

1. They create artificial systems with arbitrary sets of rules. When the learners agree to participate, they also agree to accept the new rules of conduct, and are free to let go of their usual ways of acting and thinking. This is both a liberating and a revealing experience. Learners in this state are more open (also vulnerable) to other ways of doing things. After all, it's only a game. It's also fun to be allowed—even forced—to be different. The participants are just following the rules.

2. When learners enter an activity or game, they are starting off fresh. Anything that has happened to them before in "real life" has no meaning here. This is a new opportunity for success.

3. Games, in particular, model what research has shown to foster learning success: *why, what, structure, responses, feedback,* and *reward.* All are embedded in games. It's not a coincidence that games facilitate learning.

4. Games and game-like activities incorporate three characteristics research has shown to stimulate learning: *challenge* (triggers an adrenalin rush, increasing alertness and attention); *fantasy* (stimulates the imagination; it is not the real world, but an intriguing one); and *curiosity* (promotes attention; what will happen next?).

How to Create a Game to Improve Learning and Performance Using the Frame-Game Approach

A frame game is any game that lends itself to being separated into two components: structure and content.

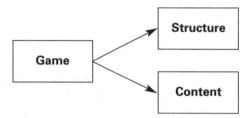

Take Bingo, for example. It consists of a structure (how the game is organized and played) and content (one- and two-digit numbers up to 75). Bingo becomes a *frame* game when you "unload" the content—the numbers—and expose its skeletal framework. You can then "reload" this framework with new content (for example, tools for carpentry, supermarket products, countries of the world). Instead of the B-I-N-G-O categories, new ones are used (for example, tools for cutting, drilling, joining, measuring. . . ; dairy, produce, meats, cleaning products. . . ; Asia, Europe, North America, South America. . .). Depending on your desired learning or performance outcome, you can adjust the play of the game, scoring system, and/or win rule. Here are the steps to create a game based on this approach:

1. Select an existing game in which rules are easy to learn or one that is familiar to most players and has a record of "attractiveness" (that is, people like to play it).
2. Unload the game's existing content and retain only its structure.
3. Reload the game with your new content. Modify the structure to accommodate your content and objectives.
4. Rewrite the game rules and procedures to match your requirements.
5. Adjust the scoring system and win rule to match your objectives and the culture of your learners.
6. Create a clever name for the game.
7. Produce rough game materials and try them out with sample learners before creating your final materials and taking the game on the road.

An example of what we mean follows. We have selected Tic-Tac-Toe as our basic frame game. We can't think of a simpler game to start with to illustrate how you can adapt a known game to become a very useful learning vehicle. Take a look at Exhibits 10-1 and 10-2, and read the explanations there. You'll see how we have taken the basic game and adapted it.

Exhibit 10-1: Traditional Tic-Tac-Toe

- Draw a 3x3 grid.
- Two players play. One selects the "X" symbol; the other, the "O" symbol.
- Players take turns placing their individual symbols, one at a time, on the grid.
- Players maneuver to line up their own symbols horizontally, vertically, or diagonally while preventing the opponent from doing the same.
- The first player to successfully line up three of his or her symbols wins.

Tic-Tac-Toe

O		X
	O	X
X	O	X

Exhibit 10-2: Adapted Game, Using Tic-Tac-Toe as the Frame

Title: What Will Get You?
Players: Adults enrolled in a consumer health education course
Objective: Name the highest-probability cause of death for specific age, race, and gender groups
Materials: • A game board on an overhead transparency as shown below:

	Black Female	Black Male	White Female	White Male
7 Years				
17 Years				
37 Years				
57 Years				

- A set of cardboard cutout X's and O's
- A summary of the current National Vital Statistics Report, which lists the top 10 causes of death for each subgroup shown in the matrix.

(continued on page 92)

Exhibit 10-2: Adapted Game, Using Tic-Tac-Toe as the Frame (continued)

Media equipment: An overhead projector and screen

Number of players: Two teams of up to seven players each. Others may serve as a TV audience and vicariously participate in the game.

Approximate time requirement: 30 minutes

Play of the game:

1. The game leader (instructor), acting as a TV host, selects two teams of players. The rest of the class applauds and generally acts as a TV audience.

2. The game leader assigns "X" to one team and "O" to the other.

3. The X team takes the first turn. It selects a cell by defining an age, race, and gender group. Team members collaboratively select what they consider to be the number-one cause of death for this particular group.

4. The opposing team may challenge the selection by offering any alternative cause that they consider to be a higher probability. One person in the audience acts as the judge. She or he has a copy of the causes of death for each of the categories in the game and, when called upon, informs everyone of the accuracy of selections.

5. If there is no challenge, the cause named by the first team must be number one. If there is a challenge, the team that is closer to number one (or is number one) wins the cell and places its symbol there.

6. Play swings back and forth between teams until one team lines up three of its symbols in a row vertically, horizontally, or diagonally and wins the game, as shown below:

	Black Female	Black Male	White Female	White Male
7 Years			X	
17 Years		X	O	O
37 Years		O	X	
57 Years		O		X

An Activity for You

Review the 25 examples in *Telling Ain't Training* (pages 115–134). Identify those games and game-like activities that you feel you can adapt, based on the frame-game approach. Add any other games or activities you know of that you feel you might want to adapt to your courses. Review the programs and/or courses in which you play a role. Identify opportunities to insert these fun, interactive designs. Build at least one activity based on the guidelines this chapter has provided. Use the template in Worksheet 10-2 to describe your new game or game-like activity.

Worksheet 10-2: Frame-Game Activity Template

Game/Activity Title:

Players/Participants:

Objective(s):

Materials/Equipment:

Number of Players/Participants:

Approximate Time Requirement:

Play of the Game/Activity *(include scoring system and/or win rule, if relevant):*

An Activity for Your Training Organization

With your team, review all of the material covered to this point in this chapter. Discuss where it would make sense to insert a game or game-like activity in your courses. Have each team identify one game opportunity and create at least one example. Do a show-and-tell to share what the teams develop. Have each team make an adaptation of another's creation for a different course or different content. Reproduce these and share all of the games/activities with all team members. As a group, you may even identify one game that could be published in the company newsletter.

Debriefing Learning Games and Game-Like Activities

There is no firm research evidence to support the claim that debriefing a highly interactive activity makes a significant difference in terms of learning or subsequent performance. But, most experienced simulation game and role-play designers/ runners believe debriefing is crucial. Debriefing models and procedures vary from one instructional context to another, but all contain a certain number of common elements. Here is one model that fits the training setting. It has been successfully used many times. It is called the D-FITGA Model to help you remember its six major debriefing phases:

1. Decompression
2. Facts
3. Inferences
4. Transfer
5. Generalizations
6. Applications

How to Debrief

The game (or game-like activity) has ended and, in the best case, lots of things have occurred during the session that have provided strong learning opportunities for the participants. How do you capture all that went on? How do you organize the mass of events, feelings, experiences, and insights into some sort of coherent form? The answer: through a carefully structured debriefing such as the six-step debriefing described below:

1. **Decompression.** During a good game or game-like activity, participants become dramatically and emotionally involved in what they are doing. They gather and process information rapidly, make decisions, test hypotheses, create strategies, and manipulate and even sometimes crush other participants. The level of involvement is high. Feelings build up and occasionally boil over. Frequently, some emotional residue remains after the activity ends. The experienced leader will help his or her group relax and decompress from the activity. Here are some decompression suggestions:

   - Call a break to allow participants to freely move around, talk, and refresh themselves.
   - Regroup the participants into an informal and comfortable seating arrangement. Let them relax.
   - Have group members close their eyes, breathe deeply, and think of dark swirling colors. Call up a pleasant image.
   - Have participants close their eyes, stretch, then relax. Have them start at the top of the head and slowly push the tensions out of their bodies through their fingers and toes.
   - Spend, in all, some three to five minutes unwinding and settling the group.

2. **Facts.** Focus your opening debriefing questions on factual information. Ask participants to recall events that occurred during the activity. Avoid

suppositions or inferences. If you have taken notes during the play of the game or the acting out of a scene, refer to these and have participants tell it their way. Below are some sample types of fact questions you could ask:

- Did anyone receive a green card? Who gave it to you? What significance did you attach to it?
- Who had more than 15 points? What strategy did you choose to get them? Did anyone make any remarks about your strategy? What did she or he say?
- When the newcomer arrived in your room, what did you do? How did you treat him or her? How did the newcomer react? Would someone who played the role of a newcomer tell us what he or she perceived on entering the room?

3. **Inferences.** When facts are established, the leader can begin questioning participants on what they thought or imagined was occurring. Questions here focus on judgment and the seeking of causes. Inferences can be confirmed or negated by other participants. All this should come out during the inferential phase of debriefing. Here are some sample debriefing questions and comments for this phase:

- Did anyone suspect that a trap was being set for him or her? What made you suspicious? What do you think was causing him to be so cautious even though you were obviously hurt?
- Why do you imagine the doctor refused assistance? Would you have done the same?
- Why do you think you were thrown out of the room? Do you think the hostile actions were justified by your conduct? Were they acting reasonably?

4. **Transfer.** In this phase, the debriefing tries to draw parallels among the events, characters, circumstances of the activity, and the participants' real work situations. Questions thus focus on comparisons between the activity and everyday life. Here are some sample questions for this transfer phase:

- Do you see any similarities between the way in which the doctor treated the victim and people or events in your work setting? How do people in authority deal with those who appear to be powerless? Or powerful?
- In the game, many of you learned the advantage of forming coalitions to survive. Would that work in your real-world setting?
- When you were punished for errors as you tried to follow directions, you soon gave up and became apathetic. Do things like this happen in real life? Give me some personal examples.
- You did your best in the other culture and still you were treated with disdain and were rejected. You began to feel hostile. Have similar events occurred for you at work? Give us an example.

5. **Generalizations.** When similarities between activity and reality have been established, the next phase is to try to create some generalizations, rules, and principles to improve or help us better understand the real world. For example,

- You felt powerless and defeated by the doctor's treatment of you. You turned resentful and uncooperative. What does that tell us about people treated this way by authority figures? What can we personally do about it?
- You saw that banding together improved the survival rate of the group. What principle can we come up with that should help us survive better in our work?
- So when you were rejected, you turned hostile. What does that tell us about tensions between different cultural groups? How do we diminish the hostility?

6. **Applications.** The final step, if it is feasible, is to lead participants to the point where they can apply generalizations, very concretely, to their own specific realities. Here are some questions:

- What will you do the next time you see abuse of authority occurring in your setting?
- You say that punishing effort decreases effort and discourages individuals from trying to solve problems. What can you do to change the punishing aspects of your work environment?
- If banding together improves the lot of everyone, what impact could that have on your situation? What can you and others do to increase cooperation and mutual assistance?

Debriefing is a fine art. It can be structured and planned, but it takes on a dynamic form of its own as participants become involved. Using a blackboard or flipchart to highlight key points, using human recorders to write down decisions that are made, and harmoniously building toward the same outcomes as the original activity sought to reach will increase the overall effect of your game or game-like learning session.

An Activity for You and Your Training Organization

Add a set of debriefing questions to at least one of the games or game-like activities you developed. Use the template presented in Worksheet 10-3. Share these questions with each other. Try out the game/game-like activity with a sample learner group. Include the debriefing. Determine what value the debriefing adds to learning.

Case Study Method

Although you have covered a great deal of training design territory in this chapter, let's add one more highly valuable tool to your growing learner-centered, performance-based tool kit: case study method. This form of learning design has demonstrated

Worksheet 10-3: D-FITGA Game Debriefing

Title of the Game:_____

1. **Decompression** (actions to create emotional distance from the game/activity)

2. **Facts** (questions focused on what occurred during the activity; only facts are allowed)

3. **Inferences** (questions focused on what participants thought, imagined, or supposed was happening—causes, reasons)

4. **Transfer** (questions aimed at drawing parallels between activity events and real life)

5. **Generalizations** (rules, principles to help us understand the real world and take actions)

6. **Applications** (questions focused on next steps)

---

itself to be wonderfully effective, especially for higher-level learning such as principle and rule application, problem analysis, decision making, planning, and creative problem solving. Case study method is also a powerful means of facilitating transfer of learning to the workplace. Let us further explore this very learner-centered design.

A case is any story-type description in which one or more decisions must be made, based on the information provided. A case can be of any length—from one short paragraph to a book. Typically cases are one to a dozen pages.

Here are the critical characteristics of a case:

*   It is a form of simulation—a representation or a slice of life, either real or hypothetical.
*   In case study method, there is a clearly defined objective to be attained associated with each case (for example, analyze and solve a job-related problem).

- Each case contains a complete, accurate description of the situation to be studied. (There is a variation of this in which cases contain partial information and learners must use other resources to obtain more input.)
- The case presents the situation clearly. The purpose is to deal with the case, not engage in reading comprehension.

Cases vary in a number of ways:

- **Purpose.** Cases may be used for instruction, evaluation, assessment, diagnosis, proficiency, maintenance, creative problem solving, organizational development, and more.
- **Length.** As mentioned earlier, a case may be as short as a paragraph or as long as a book. However, typically a case is one to a dozen pages.
- **Level of detail.** This depends on the objective of the case. Generally speaking, the more technical the content and objective (for example, troubleshoot a high-availability information technology system), the more detailed the case. A rule of thumb in developing cases is "less is more." Provide the leanest amount of information that is both necessary and sufficient for learners to deal with the case.
- **Individual or group involvement.** You can develop and use cases for single users, pairs, teams, multiple teams, and even large groups.
- **Type of conclusion.** There can be a textbook solution—the one and only right answer—or multiple acceptable solutions. In some cases, the solution is whatever a team or group agrees to by consensus.

Why Use Case Study Method?

Use of cases is excellent for marrying theory to practice. Cases bring to life processes, principles, theoretical models, even notions. Case study method also offers opportunities for practice in identifying, analyzing, and solving problems. Because the method makes use of multiple cases illustrating in ever-increasing levels of complexity a variety of theoretical notions, learners receive numerous opportunities to practice their analytical and problem-solving skills. Cases also bring to bear diverse viewpoints. The richness of ideas and confrontations of perspectives focused on a central issue greatly enhances participant learning. Finally, as stated above, cases are examples of past or potential realities. Cases bring learners closer to what they may face than do lectures or reading. This facilitates transfer and application to the workplace. To illustrate, Exhibit 10-3 contains a brief case used with bus drivers learning how to manage diversity aboard their buses.

How Do You Build Cases?

Cases are relatively easy to create. All you need to do is follow three principles and apply seven steps. The three principles are

1. Focus each case on a single issue.

Exhibit 10-3: Sample Case for Teaching Bus Drivers to Handle Diversity

A bus is travelling along Park Avenue at 2:30 on a hot summer afternoon. There are 15 people on the bus. Everything is going smoothly until, suddenly, between stops, a woman passenger runs up the aisle shouting that someone is molesting her. The driver stops the bus and follows the woman back to her seat. She points to a man who appears to be of Middle-Eastern descent, about 40 years old. She explains in an agitated, hostile manner that while there are plenty of seats on the bus, this man chose to sit down beside her. She explains that she had asked him politely to give her some room—that he was sitting too closely. He had not responded. Another woman backs up the story of the distressed woman. The middle-aged man who is the subject of the commotion doesn't seem to understand what is going on. The driver questions him about the situation, but he receives no reply. The driver orders the offending passenger to change seats. When the passenger doesn't respond, the driver physically moves him to a seat far away from the other passengers.

Questions
1. Did the driver make the right decision? Did the driver make the wrong decision? Support your conclusion.
2. What would you do in the same situation? Explain why.

---

2. Provide all necessary information to arrive at a conclusion.
3. In general, develop a series of single-issue cases that build skills over time.

Follow these seven steps:

1. For each case, select a single topic or issue. Each selection must illustrate one or a very few clearly defined principles (see Exhibit 10-4, page 100, for an example of this).
2. Collect all necessary documentation or content to make your case "authentic."
3. Create an outline for the case.
4. Identify the characters.
5. Write up the case. Make it clear, concise, and coherent. Write simply. Add dialogue as appropriate.
6. End with clear instructions on what the case user is to do.
7. Select a title. Keep it brief and specific. Don't imply a conclusion (for example, "Never Give a Loan on Faith").

The two cases in the exhibits illustrate many of the points stated in the seven steps for successful case development and writing.

When you have created a case, test it against the checklist in Worksheet 10-4, on page 100.

Running Cases in Case Study Method

The key to using cases is to get learners involved as quickly as possible. One of the most effective means for doing this is to place learners in teams, each with an elected or appointed facilitator and, if necessary, one or two "secretaries" to record findings, decisions, and conclusions. Then,

- distribute materials to all participants.
- provide sufficient time for them to review/analyze the case.

- review case requirements—the mission to be accomplished.
- facilitate discussion of the goal. Provide a "guide sheet" to team facilitators that directs them to
  - invite dialogue
  - get everyone to speak
  - summarize key points

Exhibit 10-4: Sample Case for Novice Supervisors—Managing Tardiness

Cheryl's coffee was getting cold. She was so engrossed in figuring out what to do about Dave that she didn't even notice.

"Darn, Dave's late for work again! I know he's one of my best order-takers, but I've got to do something about his tardiness. Everybody really likes him—including me. He's got such a great personality that he just seems to get by being late. How do you get mad at Dave?

"I've joked several times with Dave in the past about his being late and I know some of the others have kidded him about it, too. He's taken all the ribbing like a good sport, but it hasn't changed his behavior much. I guess one of the problems is that his being late isn't really all that bad, because he always gets his work done. His orders are always perfect. But, it's beginning to affect the rest of the order-takers. It's gone to the point that when someone else comes in late and I say something, they get really insulted and make scenes.

"'Look at Dave's time log,' they say. 'He's been late three times in a row and five times this month.' It's just out of hand. I've got to do something!"

- Determine the exact nature of the problem.
- Determine what the possible causes are for persistent tardiness. How can you verify these?
- Decide what policies and procedures are required to handle such circumstances and how these should be applied.
- What course of action should Cheryl follow with Dave? With others?

Worksheet 10-4: Criteria for a Good Case

- ☐ Clear, single topic or issue
- ☐ All necessary content and/or data included
- ☐ Characters, if any, clearly identified
- ☐ Concise, coherent; writing is tight
- ☐ Dialogue, if any, is appropriate
- ☐ Clear instructions for user—what to do
- ☐ Title is specific but does not give away conclusion
- ☐ Relevant to job
- ☐ Authentic: realistic, credible, valid
- ☐ Requires immediate resolution
- ☐ Complete: total, self-contained situation

- ensure that key points, decisions, and conclusions are recorded
- manage emotions
- not allow any individual to dominate
- manage time
- draw out consensus solution(s)
- come to a conclusion.

Bring everyone together at the end of the case discussions and debrief, using the D-FITGA debriefing model or a suitable adaptation.

An Activity for You

Identify a course for which you have responsibility—one that would benefit by including cases. The cases should replace or bring to life existing lecture or reading content. Create several cases, following the guidelines, and test these with a sample group. You will be amazed at how easy it is to do and how rapidly your learners take over the learning process. Build in a strong debriefing for each case.

An Activity for Your Training Organization

When you have tried out the case study method, bring it to the attention of your training/learning team. Share the content of this chapter with them. Try out a sample case as a group, either the one in Exhibit 10-4 from the novice supervisory program or one you created. Then, have pairs of your colleagues select a course or module and create cases that bring it to life. Try out sample cases that training group pairs develop. Share the successful ones with appropriate others.

Chapter Summary

This has been a long and, as we promised, an active chapter. As you went through it,

- you revisited the four approaches to training introduced in chapter 8 of *Telling Ain't Training* and, based on a job aid for the four approaches, you examined the training programs for which you have responsibility. You verified what the best training approach would be for each program.
- you were encouraged to share the job aid matrix with the rest of your team. They, in turn, reviewed their curricula, courses, and modules, and determined whether those were employing optimal approaches. If not, they decided what might be done to achieve the best approach.
- you reviewed the 25 activities in chapter 8 of *Telling Ain't Training* and then stepped beyond those into the world of frame games and game-like activities. After discovering a method for generating highly interactive, learner-centered activities, you were encouraged to design one or more yourself.
- you took the activities and frame-design approach to your training organization. They generated additional relevant activities and shared these.

- ◆ you acquired a model for debriefing highly participatory sessions (the D-FITGA debriefing model), developed a debriefing for one of your own interactive activities, and then shared it with your team.
- ◆ you explored cases and the case study method. You created cases, as did your colleagues, and you built in structured debriefings to elicit maximum learning.

What a great deal of activity! But did they learn? Can they apply the new learning? These are the central questions of the next chapter on testing.

Note

1. Clark, R.C. (1998). *Building Expertise: Cognitive Methods for Training and Performance Improvement.* Washington, DC: International Society for Performance Improvement.

Testing or Examining: What's the Difference?

This chapter

- announces right at the start the *Telling Ain't Training* view of testing: a positive activity for fostering learning and learner confidence
- returns to declarative and procedural knowledge concepts as a base for selecting and creating appropriate test items
- provides guidance in developing test (or learning check) items that perfectly match objectives
- details the difference between performance tests and written/oral, memory-type tests
- explains the difference between testing and certification, and describes various levels of certification.

Tools in this chapter include

- a test item decision table—a job aid that helps you select the right type of test item for a given objective
- a written test checklist—a tool for ensuring that your written tests are correctly designed
- a certification requirements and levels table, with entries arranged from lowest to highest level of certification type and with examples at each level.

Chapter 9 of *Telling Ain't Training* presents a great number of guidelines and tools for testing learning. To review two of the critical points in that chapter, remember that to support and enhance learning, testing in the form of "learning checks" can be very helpful. Testing in a learner-centered, performance-based context is the act of verifying the attainment of an objective. It is a means for determining whether the learner has accomplished what she or he set out to achieve. It provides valued and valuable information to the learner, the instructor (if there is one), and the learning system that can now offer new paths on which the learner may embark.

Testing is an opportunity to get out of the learner's way, enable her or him to solo and momentarily bask in the glow of success, especially if you organized the conditions for learning effectively.

Exams, on the other hand, come trailing clouds of discomfort. They connote some form of ordeal or trial. They are formal; their consequences can be threatening. For many adult learners, the thought of an exam is enough to trigger a high level of anxiety, resulting either in avoidance or in performance that does not adequately reflect their true capabilities.

We are strong advocates of frequent testing—learning-check activities that challenge the learner and demonstrate learning victory. The keys to effective testing are the selection of the appropriate type of test item and creation of the test item itself. Test items must perfectly match the objectives. Let's start our testing journey by taking a step backward to some learning fundamentals.

Declarative and Procedural Knowledge: A Reprise

Recall these two types of knowledge:

1. **declarative:** state, describe, explain—*talk-about* knowledge
2. **procedural:** use, apply—*do* knowledge.

If your memory of these is vague (in other words, if you are experiencing a lapse in declarative knowledge), then either return to *Telling Ain't Training* (pages 32–35) or to chapter 6 of this *Fieldbook* for a quick refresher. Examine each objective you have developed for your training and decide whether it requires declarative or procedural knowledge. Then apply the decision table in Worksheet 11-1 to select your test item.

Here's a simple example of how to use the worksheet. The objective is "Given a diagram of a rectangle and its dimensions, calculate the area using the correct formula with 100 percent accuracy."

- ◆ **Question 1:** Is this objective aimed at developing declarative knowledge or procedural knowledge? [*Answer:* procedural—*apply/do* knowledge.]
- ◆ **Question 2:** Does the learner have to perform a covert (nonvisible) task or perform an overt (externally verifiable) task? [*Answer:* perform an overt task.]

So the type of test item you should select is a performance test with a verification instrument to help check if the learner performed correctly. Now you have to select your verification instrument. In most but certainly not all cases, a behavior checklist suffices. Quickly review your choices from the worksheet and make your selection:

- ◆ *Behavior checklist:* list of correct behaviors (and often results)
- ◆ *Behavior measurement scale:* list of behaviors and a scale of how well each was done

- *Behavior frequency observation checklist:* a record of how often something was done
- *Behavior observation scale:* evaluation of how appropriate the behavior was
- *Best responses:* declaration of which behavior was best.

Worksheet 11-1: Test Item Decision Table

If the objective aims at developing . . .	And the learner has to . . .	Then select this type of test item . . .	But, beware because . . .
Declarative knowledge	Recognize the correct answer	Binary test: Offers the learner two choices to select from, only one of which is correct (for example yes/no, true/false)	• Limits answer options to two choices • There is a 50 percent chance of getting the right answer by guessing
		Matching test: Requires the learner to match an item in one column with an item in a second column. Items in the second column are usually in random order. Often, to increase challenge, there are more items in the second column than in the first.	• Restricted only to content in which pairing is feasible • Only tests low-level learning • Correct guesswork increases through a reduced range of alternatives as items are selected from the second column
		Multiple-choice test: Requires the learner to select the correct answer to a question from an array of three or four alternatives.	• Generally limited to fact-based questions • Does not allow for elaboration and/or explanation of answer • Takes skill to design well • Can become a reading/logic exercise
	Recall (retrieve from memory) the correct answer	Completion test: Requires from the learner one- or several-word answers that complete a statement. The range of acceptable completion responses is limited.	• Cannot readily be used for "how" or "why" questions • The question itself may provide clues to the correct response • Unless worded in "acceptable" fashion, it is difficult to correct mechanically; even more difficult if responses are handwritten
		Short-answer, closed-question test: Requires the learner to write or enter a briefly worded, limited response.	• Short answers limit richness of learner response • Takes longer to correct than binary, matching, multiple-choice, or completion items • Variability of responses increases in this type of test
		Open-ended essay test: Requires an extended response that can also include learner's opinion, interpretation, and vision.	• Requires strong subject-matter knowledge to verify and give feedback • Correction is labor intensive • Allows highly diverse responses, thereby subjecting correction to threat of bias or lack of comprehension • Excellent writing skills may mask lack of knowledge

(continued on page 106)

Worksheet 11-1: Test Item Decision Table (continued)

If the objective aims at developing . . .	And the learner has to . . .	Then select this type of test item . . .	But, beware because . . .
Procedural knowledge	Perform a covert task (something you cannot see being done, something that takes place in the learner's head)	A written or oral test that asks the learner to describe or explain what she or he did mentally. Use a checklist to rate whether the learner performed the mental task correctly.	• You may need to probe, especially if the learner performed parts of the tasks automatically (without conscious processing).
	Perform an overt task (something you can see being done, something externally verifiable)	A performance test with one of the following verification instruments:	
		Behavior checklist: Provides an observer with a list of behaviors the learner must demonstrate during the test.	• Limits qualitative evaluation, especially for higher levels of complex performance • Does not work well where there is a wide range of acceptable behaviors • If poorly designed, results in a high degree of observer subjectivity
		Specific behavior measurement scale: Provides an observer with a set of specific behaviors to verify and a measurement scale for each.	• Takes longer to create than a checklist • Confined only to behaviors on the scale • Can be subjective
		Behavior frequency observation checklist: Provides an observer with a checklist that helps monitor frequency of relevant and irrelevant behaviors.	• Does not verify improvement in a behavior • Requires considerable training and practice of observers to capture frequency
		Behavior observation scale: Enables an observer to judge the appropriateness of using a behavior. When a variety of behaviors have been learned, each suited to a specific situation, this permits verification of the match between situation and behavior.	• Very dependent on the ability of the observer to judge the appropriateness of a behavior
		Effectiveness checklist: Enables an observer to determine the effectiveness of a learner's behavior. It focuses on results or outcomes. What is recorded is the effect of the behavior, not the behavior itself.	• No attention to the actual learner behavior • Does not indicate how the result was achieved • Does not verify the cost of achieving the result
		Best responses: Allows for identification of the best choice of several acceptable responses or solutions.	• Does not consider different ability levels • Can be highly subjective

Because you have to use the correct formula (yes/no), correctly calculate (yes/no), and attain 100 percent accuracy (yes/no), the *behavior checklist* fits best.

Putting it all together, here's an illustration of what you might create as a test item:

Performance Objective

Given a diagram of a rectangle and its dimensions, calculate the area using the correct formula with 100 percent accuracy.

Test Item (Performance Test)

Calculate the area of this rectangle. Show the formula and your calculation.

8 feet

3 feet

Verification Checklist

	Yes	No
Formula correct	☐	☐
Calculation correct	☐	☐
Answer correct	☐	☐

You can then use the Test Item Verification job aid from *Telling Ain't Training* (Checklist 9-1, page 155) to make sure that your test item perfectly met the objective. We have included this job aid here for easy access (Exhibit 11-1, page 108).

Performance Tests

Most performance tests more or less mirror what learners are expected to do back on the job. Therefore, it is easy to camouflage testing by presenting it as a "practical exercise," a "hands-on activity," or simply a "lab" or "practice session." You can even say, following the instruction, "Now that we have seen how this is done, let's try it out ourselves. Here is a challenge for you. I'll come around to observe and, only if necessary, assist you. . . ." Low threat, but still a learning check—a form of testing.

Written Tests

This type of testing can also be presented in the guise of exercises, but it is more difficult to do so. We strongly recommend keeping written testing to a minimum for two reasons:

1. Tests create anxiety. As we pointed out earlier, this anxiety may stimulate some learners to perform well, but may also engender stress and result in some of your adult learners not performing as well as they actually can.
2. Written tests also test writing ability, logical guesswork, and reading comprehension. The results of this type of testing may not adequately reflect what some of your learners really know.

Exhibit 11-1: Test Item Verification Job Aid		

Apply the checklist below to each test item, whether it is oral or written or is a performance measure. Line up each test item with its corresponding objective. For every test item, answer each question.	**Yes**	**No**
1. Does the item require the exact same performance and standards stated in the objective?	☐	☐
2. Is the learner performance in the item verifiable?	☐	☐
3. Is the type of item selected the most appropriate one for verifying objective attainment?	☐	☐
4. Is there an answer key, a correction checklist, or a verification instrument for the item?	☐	☐
5. Are all resources required to respond to the item available to the learner?	☐	☐
If you checked off even one "no," the item does not match the objective perfectly. Rework the item until you can check off every "yes" for it.		

If you do have to create written tests, use Worksheet 11-2 to help reduce most of the common pitfalls of written testing. The checklist is based on the guidelines for written tests in *Telling Ain't Training* (page 154).

An Activity for You

Select one of the courses or modules for which you have some responsibility. Examine the objectives and learning checks/test items. Can they be improved? If yes, use the material in this chapter, especially the tools, to make them more instructionally sound.

An Activity for Your Training Organization

Very thoroughly review chapter 9 of *Telling Ain't Training* because testing is an important issue in adult learning. Summarize key concepts and practical points from the chapter and present these to your group. Share the tools this *Fieldbook* chapter has provided. In pairs or small teams, have your training group review current tests attached to or integrated within your courses. Using the concepts and tools you have shared with them, critique as a group how you test your learners. Create a list of suggested changes. Then have the pairs or teams revise the learning checks or tests for a module or course. Debrief results as a group. Show and tell "before" and "after" examples of learning checks and/or tests.

Testing and Certification

We close this chapter with a note of caution regarding *testing* and *certification*. Although there is some relationship between these two terms, each carries so many different connotations for individuals and organizations that confusion often results. For us, testing is no more than a means for verifying objective attainment.

Worksheet 11-2: Written Test Checklist

	Yes	No
1. The test items match course objectives perfectly.	☐	☐
2. The test starts with a few "easy questions" to reduce test anxiety.	☐	☐
3. Test items are written at language and reading levels appropriate to the learners.	☐	☐
4. There are few negatives and no double negatives in question items.	☐	☐
5. Test items are concise, precise, and unambiguous.	☐	☐
6. Test items are not simply repetitions of statements in a learning manual that demand memorization rather than comprehension.	☐	☐
7. No test item includes clues about other test items.	☐	☐
8. There are no trick test items that encourage guessing over comprehension.	☐	☐
9. If different types of test items are used (for example, binary, multiple-choice, and completion), same-type questions are grouped together to reduce the number of instructions and facilitate the learners' tasks.	☐	☐
10. There are examples to illustrate how to respond to complex types of questions.	☐	☐
11. There are clear instructions to instructors and/or learners concerning length of test and rules for test taking and test administration.	☐	☐
12. Test items have been tried out and revised prior to implementation.	☐	☐
A "no" for any item should trigger a revision or require a valid reason for accepting the "no."		

Given what the learner was supposed to be able to do, either declaratively or procedurally, and how well she or he was to do it, did she or he succeed? A "yes" answer triggers confirmation to the learner. A "no" response generates corrective feedback to help the learner achieve the desired result.

All of that assumes you have conducted a proper task analysis; developed performance objectives derived directly from the learner-centered, performance-based task analysis; and created test items (or learning checks) that perfectly match these items. The items are the best (or most feasible) for the learner and the objectives. The testing conditions are the most appropriate.

If all of these requirements have been met and the learners demonstrate performance capability as specified in the objectives, then you can "certify" their ability to perform. However, all *certification* means is that they can do what the objectives require—no more. Why this limitation? Because others may assume that your certification implies more than this. Learners who succeed in a course or program may be able to meet the objectives, but without real-world practice, they may still be awkward or slow at performing. Being able to resuscitate a "dummy" in a CPR class and actually doing it live at a dockside fire are very different situations. To what extent is the certification, despite prior testing, valid?

This leads to interpretations of the term *certification*. We have established some arbitrary levels of certification in Table 11-1 to illustrate what we mean. Obviously, there are endless variations of these levels, including ones that are more or less rigorous in their certification process. We have not dealt with *licensing* here, which encompasses specific professional groups, such as medical doctors, lawyers, psychologists, accountants, and others who may not practice legally without passing through a rigorous certification ordeal.

Our purpose in bringing the issue of testing and certification to your attention is to recommend caution in the use of these two terms. Testing is one thing; certification another. We urge prudence in considering how to link the two practices and precision in how you apply and communicate your training organization's practices in each case.

Chapter Summary

This testing chapter, although not especially long, covered a number of practices and issues that are not only intimately linked with training, but that profoundly affect the impact and influence of your training organization. Let's recall what you did:

- ◆ You reviewed the distinction between testing (a practice to verify objective attainment) and exams (a more formal and often threatening experience).
- ◆ You revisited declarative and procedural knowledge in the testing context and, using a test item decision table, you selected the most appropriate test items for given objectives. You applied a second test to verify whether a test item perfectly matched its performance-based objective.
- ◆ You examined a written test checklist designed to help reduce common written test pitfalls.
- ◆ You and your training colleagues revisited existing courses/modules and their tests in order to improve the way in which you test your learners.
- ◆ You gave us an opportunity to present both information and concerns about the loose way in which testing and certification practices are employed in too many workplace organizations. We sincerely hope you took our cautions to heart.

Because testing is not only a powerful training technique, but also one fraught with misuse, we urge you to examine within your work setting how tests are created, validated, and applied. Make sure that tests are derived from performance objectives directly related to the learner's work and the organization's needs and goals. Establish clear guidelines with respect to testing and certification. Remember, the purposes of the test, above all, are to prove and to *help improve* learner performance capability.

A fine resource to assist you with your testing efforts is *Criterion-Referenced Test Development: Technical and Legal Guidelines for Corporate Training and Certification*,

Table 11-1: Levels of Certification

Type of Requirement	Certification Level	Examples
• Pay a fee; receive a certificate	I	• Become a registered clergyman of the Church of the Free Spirits. Send $100. • Receive your master's degree in business administration. No coursework required. Send check to the University of Gullibility.
• Attend a program; receive a certificate	II	• Attend a three-day workshop on a new medical procedure. No testing required. • Enroll in an online cartoonist program. Complete the eight modules and receive your "cartoonist's certification." Anyone can succeed! Just buy all eight modules and let us know when you have finished them.
• Attend a program and pass the written test[a]	III	• Complete a software technician course to become certified in a certain program or operating system. Test has 100 multiple-choice items. • Take a sales course on a specific pharmaceutical product. You must pass the written test.
• Attend a program and pass both written and practical tests	IV	• Complete a software technician course to become certified in a certain program or operating system. Certification requires success on written, practical application, and problem-solving/troubleshooting tests. • Take a sales course on a specific pharmaceutical product. You must pass a written test on the product. You must also demonstrate making a presentation of the product to specialist physicians and responding to their questions (simulation role plays).
• Attend a program, pass both written and practical tests, and formally demonstrate on-job performance over a specified time period (or submit valid evidence of real-world performance) to a defined standard	V	• Complete a financial management program for certified financial managers or advisors with oversight from a professional society that includes qualified and experienced inspectors. • Complete an electronics technician program with various grade levels, delivered and/or administered by a recognized institution with field examiners.

a. This type of certification is a "tricky" one. The testing portion implies performance capability. The caution here is that written tests generally require declarative knowledge. The real world requires procedural knowledge and capability. The validity of explaining how to do something or selecting the right multiple-choice option as a representation of ability to perform can be suspect. Watch out here.

2d ed., by S. A. Shrock, W. C. Coscarelli, and P. Eyres (Washington, DC: International Society for Performance Improvement, 2000).

You have come a long distance beyond *Telling Ain't Training*. You have had much to do and acquired a large number of tools along the way.

Now for a change of pace. Chapter 10 of *Telling Ain't Training* devoted itself to training myths and lore. In the next chapter of this *Fieldbook,* we revisit those dozen myths, but with a focus on application in your workplace.

Chapter 12

Hit or Myth:
What's the Truth?

This chapter

- ◆ reviews a dozen myths debunked in *Telling Ain't Training*, adds recommendations for countering each one, and triggers actions on your part
- ◆ builds a case for you and your training organization to align your actions with the suggestions of well-researched evidence.

Tools in this chapter include

- ◆ a hit-or-myth applications table that restates each myth, succinctly presents research findings, makes recommendations, and calls for action from you and your organization.

Applying folk remedies to an ailment often does a great deal of harm. Although science sometimes uncovers value in a limited number of these traditional cures (for example, chicken soup does help when you have a cold; leeches can remove certain body toxins), there are inherent dangers in most of them. In some cases people have suffered severe consequences from their application.

Without overdramatizing the point, you, as a concerned professional, have a responsibility. It is to wisely use limited organizational resources to help your learners and the training organization achieve performance results that they and all other stakeholders value. Your responsibility includes setting aside unsubstantiated training lore. The purpose of chapter 10 in *Telling Ain't Training* was to help you do this. Based on the dozen myths that book presented, let's proceed beyond their presentation to your own on-job application.

Worksheet 12-1: Hit or Myth Applications (page 114) is designed with this in mind. The first column presents each myth, and the second establishes what science and research have shown to be the truth. Column three offers guidelines for what you should consider doing in your organizational situation. That leaves the last column, *Actions.* This is *your* territory. We urge you to list one or two actions that you can take to bring the guidelines to life for each myth.

Worksheet 12-1: Hit or Myth Applications

Myth Statement	Research Findings	Recommendations	Actions
1—Experts who perform well generally know what they are doing and are the best people to explain their successes.	• Experts often cannot articulate the knowledge they use when demonstrating expertise. • Experts can explain what they are doing in a specific case, but cannot recommend general principles to apply across all cases. • Experts possess great amounts of procedural knowledge, but not necessarily the declarative knowledge to explain what they know.	• Use experts as an information source, but do not expect them to teach what they know in ways learners will understand. • Observe the expert in action. Probe to discover thought processes and reasons for decisions/actions. • Use experts to review learning materials for accuracy, currency, completeness, and, if appropriate, job relevance. • Use experts to generate real-world scenarios, examples, and problems, and to review learner solutions.	
2—Because some learners are more visual and others more auditory, this is key for effective learning.	• Although research has shown there to be differences in which senses individuals favor for attending to and learning from, this is less important than stimulus variation. • The importance of addressing a more favored sense is small compared with structure, response, feedback, and use of multisensory stimulation.	• Do not be overly concerned about sensory differences. Address several senses in an integrated fashion. • Vary stimulation to maintain attention and learner interest. • Concentrate on what helps all learners learn——the universals of learning research.	
3—The more enjoyable the instructional methods, the greater the learning achievement.	• Correlations vary between enjoyment and learning—some quite dramatically, from highly positive to equally negative. • Enjoyment and satisfaction are not the critical variables for learning. Persistence/time on task appears more powerful. • Also powerful are meaningfulness and mental engagement.	• Although learning can be made enjoyable, focus more on challenge to the learners and on means for extending persistence at the learning task. • Make learning personally beneficial and meaningful to learners. • Develop activities that consistently engage your learners mentally.	

Myth Statement	Research Findings	Recommendations	Actions
4—All other things being equal, media make a major difference in learning effectiveness.	• One of the most consistent research findings is that when content is held stable, media have not shown superiority among themselves or over conventional training modes with respect to learning effectiveness. • Key differences in learning are related to the instructional designs embedded in the media. • Media can increase access to learning; reduce cost with large, dispersed learner populations; and permit rapid revisions. These are learning efficiency issues.	• Use media with caution. Focus on learning access and efficiencies, not effectiveness. • Apply the same research-based learning principles (for example, meaningfulness, mental engagement, active responding, feedback) to mediated learning as you do to live instruction. • Adapt the instructional designs to maximally exploit media characteristics.	
5—Working out problems on your own results in better problem-solving performance than does studying those problems that have already been worked out.	• Learners studying worked-out problems and their solutions solve problems better in initial stages of learning. • Studying model solutions lightens cognitive load and increases problem-solving success.	• Provide learners in initial stages of learning how to solve problems with worked-out solutions to study before they embark on actual problem solving. • As more complex problems are introduced, provide model solutions initially.	
6—The more content you give to learners, the more they take away.	• Human ability to process information is limited. Too much content overloads working memory and decreases learning. • Disconnected learning material, not associated with prior knowledge, is poorly retained. • Chunked and meaningful packets of learning content increase the efficiency of learning, retention, and retrieval.	• Less is more. Include less, but highly relevant learning content. • Provide less information and more practice. • Chunk information into meaningful learning packets (for example, mnemonics, visual clusters, or rhymes). • Use analogies, image-rich comparisons, and metaphors to build bridges between prior knowledge and new learning.	

(continued on page 116)

Worksheet 12-1: Hit or Myth Applications (continued)

Myth Statement	Research Findings	Recommendations	Actions
7—A well-designed training program will overcome a poor implementation plan.	• Training has low impact if there is no time to take the training; if resources for learning are insufficient; if there is no pre- or post-training support, no incentive to learn or apply learning to the job; if there are no policies and/or procedures to integrate newly acquired learning.	• Conduct a careful context analysis to determine what will support effective training implementation. • Build sound implementation infrastructures. • Encourage supervisors to support their learners before and after training. • Ensure that incentives are in place to encourage learning and post-training application.	
8—Technology is the key to future workplace training success.	• Technology amplifies and speeds up. It does not transform poor design into effective learning. • Like media, technology affects access, cost, and currency but not learning effectiveness.	• Use technology to facilitate training/learning implementation. • Use technology to build virtual environments for learning, but apply the same research-based principles to foster learning that you apply to live learning contexts.	
9—Lack of workplace performance is mostly due to a lack of required skills or knowledge.	• Many other factors affect workplace performance: lack of clear expectations; limited access to required information, resources; poor incentives or consequences; inadequate feedback; poor selection of people to perform tasks; and many other environmental factors. • Environmental factors account for most of the issues of performance deficiency.	• Analyze before developing training solutions. • Identify the issues of a performance gap to determine whether lack of skills or knowledge—the only reason to train—is among them. • Focus on the environment and its support of performance before turning to training as an intervention.	
10—Successful performance during training usually results in improved performance on the job.	• Rarely is training sufficient to achieve sustained, improved post-training performance. • Support from supervisors and specialists helps a great deal. • Control of a number of environmental factors is necessary. The major factors are information, resources, incentives, consequences, selection, communication, process design, and task interferences.	• Think systemically—think of integrated performance solutions to ensure post-training, on-job application. • Organize the environment to support learners' application of learning from training to the job. • Build in motivational components to trigger commitment to apply, engagement on the job, and persistence once engaged.	

Myth Statement	Research Findings	Recommendations	Actions
11—To promote transfer of training to the job, focus primarily on post-training variables.	• What happens before training has a significant impact on post-training application of learning. • Selecting trainees who have no chance of applying their learning to the job wastes resources and results in little or no transfer. • If supervisors prepare learners for training, the learners' motivation to apply their learning increases. • When training design includes analysis of job requirements and then builds job-relevant tools and practice into the training, there is greater transfer.	• Support supervisors with materials and scripts they can use to prepare learners prior to training. • Select for training only those workers who will be able to apply what they learn to the job. • Devote adequate time and resources to analyze job requirements prior to training, develop job-relevant tools, and create sufficient practice activities to build capability in using the tools. Create realistic situations for the practice sessions.	
12—Good, old-fashioned common sense is a natural friend of science. It is a sure guide for making sound training decisions.	• Research textbooks all cite *common sense* as one of the greatest enemies of science. • Common sense is in the eye of the beholder who selects data to support preconceived notions. • Despite research findings, many training enthusiasts inflict practices on learners even when there is evidence of no or even negative impact.	• Be vigilant in identifying training myths. Find data or respectable evidence to counter them. • Read well-documented articles and reports on learning and performance. • Do not engage in training practices that have been fueled by enthusiasm without evidence of effectiveness. Seek proof. • Be a researcher. Evaluate, measure, and select hard evidence for your endeavors.	

An Activity for You

Examine each myth statement in Worksheet 12-1 and read the associated content in the second and third columns. Reflect on your work, your learners, and your work content. Enter at least one action you can take to better align your training practices with what is recommended. If you are already doing the right things, note this to reward yourself. Cite evidence or an example.

When you've finished the worksheet, bravo for you! This is a great step forward. Separating oneself from dearly held myths is difficult. Collecting data and research evidence is not everyone's idea of having fun. Nevertheless, advancing in this direction is more than worthwhile. It is essential for a truly effective learning and performance support system. By engaging in the actions you have noted above, you emerge as a training leader.

An Activity for Your Training Organization

Having reviewed Worksheet 12-1, you are ready to introduce this theme to your group. Review the 12 hit-or-myth statements in *Telling Ain't Training* (pages 161–166) and have your group decide whether each is a hit or a myth. Debrief with the group, using the content provided for each statement. Then share Worksheet 12-1 with everyone. As a team, decide on actions your training organization can take to reduce myth-based training and align it with what research on learning and performance suggests. A next step is to decide how to operationalize these actions.

Chapter Summary

This chapter had you do the following things:

- ◆ You examined a hit-or-myth applications worksheet in which you reviewed 12 training myths and, based on recommendations for avoiding these, generated actions you can take as a training professional and leader.
- ◆ You shared the hit-or-myth challenge with your group and together identified actions your training organization should initiate to reduce myth-based training and align itself with what science recommends.

Your progress has been remarkable. Now you're ready to launch yourself as a learner-centered, performance-based organization with a mission to apply what scientific research recommends to improve learning and achieve valued outcomes. Your action plan going forward is not only to make this happen, but also to ensure that the direction and drive persist. The next chapter on professional development will provide assistance with this.

Chapter 13

Beyond *Telling Ain't Training:* Ongoing Growth and Development

This chapter

- ◆ returns to the start of the *Beyond Telling Ain't Training Fieldbook* and asks you and your training organization to assess again where you are and where you desire to be on seven *Telling Ain't Training* dimensions
- ◆ presents the three Cs of professionalism in training
- ◆ recommends and offers guidelines for setting up a support system for your environment
- ◆ helps you diagnose facilitating and inhibiting factors in moving from telling to training
- ◆ helps you exploit facilitating factors and eliminate inhibiting ones
- ◆ offers you a training observation system to monitor trainer behaviors
- ◆ offers you a continuous improvement system for building training capabilities via video practice sessions
- ◆ recommends and suggests ways of forming a *Telling Ain't Training* study group.

Tools in this chapter include

- ◆ a *Telling Ain't Training* individual evaluation, identical to the one you encountered in chapter 2 and, as promised, presented here for you to use in reassessing yourself
- ◆ a *Telling Ain't Training* evaluation of your training organization, also identical to the one in chapter 2 for the same reasons
- ◆ an Ideas for Building a Support System worksheet to help you create ways to support your progress toward becoming the training organization you want to have
- ◆ a Support System Action Plan to make sure you actually develop an effective support system
- ◆ a Personal Facilitating and Inhibiting Factors template to help you sort through what will help you grow and develop and what potentially can hold you back

◆ a Personal Action Plan to Enhance Facilitating Factors and Decrease Inhibiting Factors worksheet

◆ an Organizational Factors Facilitating and Inhibiting Progress Toward Our Goal worksheet, which can help your team isolate systemic elements that can either help or hinder team advancement

◆ an Organizational Action Plan to Enhance Facilitating Factors and Decrease Inhibiting Factors worksheet

◆ a Trainer Observation and Feedback form to help your trainers enhance their training skills

◆ a Video Practice Session Observation Checklist, which can be used to provide feedback to trainers engaged in structured videotaped practice activities.

In chapter 2 of this *Fieldbook* you and your training group had an opportunity to conduct a *Telling Ain't Training* self-assessment. The instrument you used had seven dimensions. You indicated where you are and where you would like to be on each dimension. Without looking back, assess yourself again now that you have had an opportunity to begin applying the principles, guidelines, and tools of both *Telling Ain't Training* and this *Fieldbook*.

We have reproduced the instructions and instruments for you here. Remember, do the individual assessment on your own first (see Assessment 13-1). Then join with your team to do the organization assessment (see Assessment 13-2, page 122). When you have finished both assessments, go back to the assessments you completed in chapter 2 and identify any differences between the two sets.

An Activity for You

Here are the instructions for completing the assessments:

1. For each dimension, read the descriptions at both ends of the continuum.
2. For each dimension, using two different colored pens or pencils, place an "X" on the continuum at those points you consider to be your own current state (one color) and your own desired state (the second color).
3. When you have placed all of your Xs in both colors, use a ruler to join all Xs in the "desired" color and then join all the Xs in the "current" color. You'll have two (probably zig-zag) vertical lines. Here is an example (current = solid line; desired = dashed line):

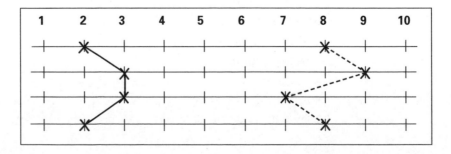

Assessment 13-1: *Telling Ain't Training* Individual Evaluation

Dimension	State A	1	2	3	4	5	6	7	8	9	10	State Z
My mission	To transmit to learners information that is accurate, up-to-date, and complete											To transform learners so that they perform in ways that they and all stakeholders value
How I am viewed by management and clients	Primarily as a deliverer of content											Primarily as an agent of performance change
My basic job	Create and/or deliver content-accurate courses											Create individuals and/or teams able to demonstrate that they achieve what is expected of them
The products and services I provide	Courses and curriculum materials											Processes, tools and sufficient practice, feedback, follow-up, and support so that learners can perform back on the job
My needs-assessment process	Take training orders from management and/or customers											Verify where knowledge and skill gaps exist and identify where and what kind of training or other forms of support should be given
My evaluation practices	Check learners' reactions to and perceptions of the training											Verify learning, transfer of learning to the job, and impact of learning on bottom-line results
My accountabilities	How well learners rate my training/courses and how many were trained											How well learners perform on the job and my contribution to bottom-line results

Assessment 13-2: *Telling Ain't Training* Organization Evaluation

Dimension	State A	1	2	3	4	5	6	7	8	9	10	State Z
Our training organization's mission	To transmit to learners information that is accurate, up-to-date, and complete											To transform learners so that they perform in ways that they and all stakeholders value
How our training organization is viewed by management and clients	Primarily as a deliverer of content											Primarily as an agent of performance change
Our training organization's basic job	Create and/or deliver content-accurate courses											Create individuals and/or teams able to demonstrate that they achieve what is expected of them
The products and services our training organization provides	Courses and curriculum materials											Processes, tools and sufficient practice, feedback, follow-up, and support so that learners can perform back on the job
Our needs-assessment process	Take training orders from management and/or customers											Verify where knowledge and skill gaps exist and identify where and what kind of training or other forms of support should be given
Our evaluation practices	Check learners' reactions to and perceptions of the training											Verify learning, transfer of learning to the job, and impact of learning on bottom-line results
Our training organization's accountabilities	How well learners rate our training/courses and how many were trained											How well learners perform on the job and our contribution to bottom-line results

4. Note the discrepancies between the two zig-zag lines. A distance of three points or more between desired and current states on any dimension suggests that you have a lot to do to move from where you are to where you want to be.

An Activity for Your Training Organization

Here are the instructions for completing the organization assessment:

1. For each dimension, read the descriptions at both ends of the continuum.

2. For each dimension, using two different colored pens or pencils, place an "X" on the continuum at the point you think should be your training organization's desired state (one color) and at the point you consider to be your training organization's current state (the second color).

3. When you have placed all of your Xs in both colors, use a ruler to join the Xs in the "desired" color and then join all the Xs in the "current" color. Again you'll have two irregular vertical lines. Here's an example (current = solid line; desired = dashed line):

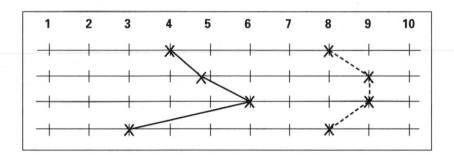

4. Note the discrepancies between the two zig-zag lines. A distance of three or more points between desired and current states suggests that your training organization has a lot to do to move from where it is to where it ought to be.

Now that you've completed the second round of assessments, did you find any significant changes either in current or desired states? We don't anticipate large changes for you, personally, with respect to the desired state, but we do hope that the current state is beginning to edge closer to what you desire, and that your training organization has progressed in its desired thinking. With time, you should experience greater convergence between current and desired states on all dimensions. Please conduct these assessments again in four to six months and then regularly two to three times each year. This will keep you thinking about what more there is that all of you can do to become a learner-centered, performance-based organization, as you would wish it to be.

Training Professionals' Three Cs

A number of years ago we heard a powerful speaker (whose name we have forgotten) expound on the three Cs of training professionals. We may have lost the name, but the ideas live on. He suggested that true training professionals possess three critical characteristics: *competence, confidence,* and *caring.* We later came to realize that the three Cs apply to virtually all workplace professionals. In our training world they certainly resonate with our values.

We are engaged in helping people in organizations perform in ways that they, the organization, and all other relevant parties value. We do this by building skills and knowledge and by supporting efforts to achieve desired performance. Here is where our three Cs connect.

1. **Competence.** Competence is the ability to perform in ways that are required by the workplace—especially the job. This is our primary concern. If we are to succeed at this, we must have the competence to develop people appropriately. This demands that we continuously study how we can do our work better, support our learners to achieve their successes, and leverage to the maximum the human capital in our organization. The maxim for this is *Hire for Characteristics; Train for Competence.* You have been hired into the training function because you have what it takes to do the job. Now you must be continually engaged in building ever-greater competence in learning and performance support.

2. **Confidence.** Self-assurance and trust in your ability to perform are necessary to help learners achieve their desired ends. Where does confidence come from? It comes from evidence of success. Confidence grows with data-based results and reliance on sound and tested work methods. Confidence building requires study, reflection, action, verification, and the accumulation of credible results. As you develop professionally, confidence in your training efforts will continue to grow—both your own confidence and that of the people who call on you.

3. **Caring.** Without deep commitment to the development and success of your learners, your training efforts will remain weak. In many organizations we have seen training activities occurring because they are expected. Managers have "training" boxes to check off. Training personnel engage in frantic activity to justify their existence. These are hollow signs of training value. Only when there is true dedication, not just to "training," but also to successful application of learning and valued results, does the total worth of what you contribute emerge. Caring often grows with a clear vision of the contribution you make to people's lives and organizational success.

Building a Support System for Your Environment

Going it alone ain't easy. Trying to become an effective training professional by yourself may simply lead to frustration. You need support to be successful within your training organization. So do your training colleagues. Here are some suggestions for building your and your group's support system (Worksheet 13-1). It is a starter list that should trigger ideas of your own.

Worksheet 13-1: Ideas for Building a Support System

Action	We Already Do It	We Can Easily Do It	This Will Take Effort	This Will Be Almost Impossible to Do, But We Can Try
1. Create a training resource library and encourage use of it.				
2. Hold in-house workshops and seminars on training issues, and have the entire group attend.				
3. Read articles, highlight key passages, copy these, and circulate them to team members and clients.				
4. Target individual, receptive clients with whom you can collaborate, build success, and then leverage results with other clients.				
5. Hold show-and-tell meetings at which you and your colleagues share training successes and difficulties with clients and management.				
6. As a team, attend professional training conferences and share what you learned with one another.				
7. Develop total-team projects that enhance professional growth (for example, calculate training's return-on-investment, develop instructor standards and then observe each other in action, create a best-practices task force).				
8. Take a senior manager to lunch to educate him or her about the training group's aspirations and potential impact on the company's bottom line. Seek support. Offer concrete suggestions.				
9. Enroll in external courses and programs related to training. Share learning and resources with others. Encourage others to enroll.				
10. Join local and national training, learning, and performance organizations (such as ASTD and ISPI). Attend meetings. Become active in local chapter events. Share what you learn.				
11. Create links to other, similar external groups in organizations both related to your industry and outside of it.				

(continued on page 126)

Worksheet 13-1: Ideas for Building a Support System (continued)

Action	We Already Do It	We Can Easily Do It	This Will Take Effort	This Will Be Almost Impossible to Do, But We Can Try
12. Establish relationships with internal and external mentors who can help you and your team develop professionally.				
13. Celebrate training and performance improvement successes that you and your team members achieve.				
14. Informally assist one another on training issues and projects. Create an informal support network.				
15. Document what works. Share the knowledge, practices, models, examples, templates, and designs with others. Develop a Website that everyone in your training group can access.				
16. Submit for professional awards if you or your group has had a successful training initiative. If you win, publicize it to build credibility and support for your endeavors.				

An Activity for You

Read through the list in Worksheet 13-1. Cross through those items that aren't feasible in your environment or don't appeal to you. Add your own actions to the list. Then put a checkmark in one of the four columns beside each item.

An Activity for Your Training Organization

Share the list of retained items (including your additions) with your group. Ask team members to delete unappealing or unfeasible ones and then to place checkmarks beside those they consider appropriate. Verify whether they place the checkmarks as you did. For each action your group retains, determine what it will take to make it happen. Prioritize the actions on the list. Then develop an action plan and schedule for each. Assign responsibilities. Worksheet 13-2: Support System Action Plan (page 128) can help with this.

Facilitating and Inhibiting Factors in Moving From Telling to Training

We all know only too well the truth of the expression, *the spirit is willing but the flesh is weak.* Progressing toward the desired state from where you are as indicated in your *Telling Ain't Training* assessment is an evolutionary process. It always takes longer than you think it should.

To reduce the time—and the obstacles—you must carefully analyze your current training environment and practices. You also have to objectively assess current competency levels, resources, expectations, and numerous other factors that can influence your practice. One way to start is to make a list of existing factors that you feel can facilitate the transformation from telling and transmission to training and transformation. Then make a list of the inhibiting factors.

An Activity for You

Start with yourself. Be totally honest. List physical, emotional, spiritual, intellectual, social, professional, personal, and other factors or issues that either facilitate or inhibit your personal transformation. Remember that forewarned is forearmed, so make each list as exhaustive as you can. Use Worksheet 13-3: Personal Factors Facilitating or Inhibiting Progress Toward My Desired State (page 129) as a template for your lists.

If you have been rigorously honest with yourself, both lists should be fairly long. Unfortunately, the inhibiting-factors column often ends up longer. Nevertheless, this is your reality. Your next step is to determine how you can go about accentuating the positive and eliminating (or at least decreasing) the negative. Worksheet 13-4: Personal Action Plan to Enhance Facilitating Factors and Decrease Inhibiting Factors (page 130) can help you do this. Exhibit 13-1, on page 131, presents several examples to trigger your own ideas.

Worksheet 13-2: Support System Action Plan

Action	Start Date	End Date	Person Responsible	Other Contributors	Resources Required

Worksheet 13-3: Personal Factors Facilitating or Inhibiting Progress Toward My Desired State

Facilitating Factors	Inhibiting Factors

Worksheet 13-4: Personal Action Plan to Enhance Facilitating Factors and Decrease Inhibiting Factors

Facilitating Factors	Actions to Enhance

Inhibiting Factors	Actions to Decrease or Eliminate

Exhibit 13-1: Sample Personal Action Plan to Enhance and Decrease Factors	

Facilitating Factors	Actions to Enhance
• New manager of training who seems to want us to improve our results • Recent best-practice study of training in our industry shows great results • Tuition reimbursement program	• Meet with manager. Show tools from this *Fieldbook* and obtain support. • Make copies, highlight key leverage points, and circulate. • Enroll in local university training certificate program.
Inhibiting Factors	**Actions to Decrease or Eliminate**
• Training budget reduced by 5 percent • Already have a heavy workload • I've got a great reputation as a "sage on the stage." I like to tell and others seem to like it too	• Show how transforming some of our current courses can save time and money. • Meet with manager to discuss current workload. Show where certain tasks can be transformed into more productive ones. • So why am I troubled? I can still do speaking, but can add to my reputation by showing fabulous learning and performance results.

An Activity for Your Training Organization

You certainly must have seen this coming. As you did for yourself, you should now extend your thinking to your training organization. Using Worksheets 13-5 and 13-6 (pages 132 and 133), work as a group to list facilitating and inhibiting factors first. Then list actions to exploit facilitating factors and eliminate or decrease inhibiting ones. If you feel it is appropriate, share your personal lists from the work you did above.

The lists and actions you and your group have generated are extremely valuable as you move forward from current to desired states. Keep these close at hand and refer to them frequently to keep up the progress. As you exploit the facilitating factors and work to reduce or eliminate the inhibiting elements, changes will occur more rapidly.

A Training Observation Instrument and Guidelines for Its Use

Part of ongoing growth and development in training is continuously improving in one's ability to help learners learn. An essential part of training is the actual delivery of learning content to learners. According to ASTD's 2004 Industry Report,[1] approximately 30 percent of training is delivered in a technology-mediated format, but almost 70 percent is still presented live by a trainer. It is essential that trainers deliver whatever has been designed (whether by themselves or others) in a learner-centered, performance-based manner, consistent with all of the principles we have put forth so far. What follows is an instrument aimed at helping trainers and instructors develop the attributes and actions of an effective "transformer." We call

Worksheet 13-5: Organizational Factors Facilitating or Inhibiting Progress Toward Our Desired State

Facilitating Factors	Inhibiting Factors

Worksheet 13-6: Organizational Action Plan to Enhance Facilitating Factors and Decrease Inhibiting Factors

Facilitating Factors	Actions to Enhance

Inhibiting Factors	Actions to Decrease or Eliminate

this instrument the Trainer Observation and Feedback Form (Worksheet 13-7). It's easy to use. Best of all, it can be employed by fellow trainers to provide guidance and feedback to one another. There are two main purposes for observing and evaluating a trainer:

1. to help the trainer improve his or her instructional effectiveness
2. to provide the trainer and the organization with a portrait of how well the trainer is performing, especially with respect to being learner-centered and performance-based.

Here is what an observer does:

1. The observer reviews the Trainer Observation and Feedback Form, deleting items that are not relevant to the specific trainer and content.
2. The observer makes sure that the trainer has received a copy of the (revised) Trainer Observation and Feedback Form and knows how it will be used.
3. The observer unobtrusively watches the trainer in action and rates her or him by circling a score on the scale (5 = excellent; 1 = poor/not at all) for each item.
4. Beside each item, the observer cites evidence and/or makes a comment to support the rating. If the observer rates an item 3 or less, she or he *must* make an explanatory comment. The observer should also make positive, congratulatory comments where suitable. The observer then notes brief suggestions for improvement.
5. When the observer has completed all ratings, she or he totals these and enters the total in the Total box at the end of the form. By dividing the total by the number of rated items, the observer produces an average rating, which is used to represent the trainer's overall performance rating.
6. Following the observation, observer and trainer meet to debrief on all rated items. The observer notes and emphasizes major strengths. The observer also makes notes and recommendations concerning areas for improvement.
7. A learner-centered, performance-based trainer should achieve an overall rating of 4.0 or higher. If there are two or more ratings of 3 or less, arrangements should be made for another observation in the near future.

By periodically employing this instrument as a feedback tool, your trainers will continuously improve their "transforming" capabilities.

An Activity for Your Training Organization

We strongly recommend sharing this instrument with your team. If you already have one that is similar, see if any of the items we have provided will add strength to what you currently use. With your group, create a process and procedures for ongoing observation and feedback.

Worksheet 13-7: Trainer Observation and Feedback Form

Trainer's Name: _____ Course: _____

Observer's Name: _____ Date: _____ Time: _____ to _____

Item	Rating Excellent → Poor/Not at All	Evidence/Comments	Suggestions
Before Training			
1. Organizes room effectively	5 4 3 2 1		
2. Finds out about participants	5 4 3 2 1		
3. Positions and tests equipment	5 4 3 2 1		
4. Prepares and sequences participant materials for distribution	5 4 3 2 1		
5. Prepares self in terms of content and materials	5 4 3 2 1		
During Instruction			
Actions			
6. Provides clear, meaningful objectives	5 4 3 2 1		
7. Verifies participants' knowledge, skills, and attitudes	5 4 3 2 1		
8. Provides clear directions and explanations	5 4 3 2 1		
9. Provides clear and relevant examples where needed	5 4 3 2 1		
10. Verifies participant learning and performance	5 4 3 2 1		
11. Provides feedback in a positive manner	5 4 3 2 1		
12. Manages instructional time effectively	5 4 3 2 1		
13. Uses instructional aids effectively	5 4 3 2 1		
14. Summarizes and concludes effectively	5 4 3 2 1		
Attributes			
15. Creates and maintains a positive learning climate	5 4 3 2 1		
16. Speaks clearly and correctly	5 4 3 2 1		
17. Uses voice dynamics effectively	5 4 3 2 1		

(continued on page 136)

Worksheet 13-7: Trainer Observation and Feedback Form (continued)

Item	Rating Excellent → Poor/Not at All	Evidence/Comments	Suggestions
18. Uses body language effectively	5 4 3 2 1		
19. Maintains proper eye contact with participants	5 4 3 2 1		
20. Maintains control of the group	5 4 3 2 1		
21. Demonstrates interest in the content	5 4 3 2 1		
22. Demonstrates interest in the participants	5 4 3 2 1		
23. Presents a neat, professional image and appearance	5 4 3 2 1		
24. Exhibits confidence	5 4 3 2 1		
Following Instruction			
25. Restores order to room for next learning session	5 4 3 2 1		
26. Removes equipment and materials no longer required	5 4 3 2 1		
27. Follows up instruction with individual participants, as needed	5 4 3 2 1		
28. Corrects participant assignments punctually and accurately	5 4 3 2 1		
29. Completes reports and paperwork punctually and correctly	5 4 3 2 1		

Total Ratings		**Number of Retained Items**		**Average Rating**	**Number of Items Rated 3 or Less**
	divided by		=		

Overall areas of strength:

Major suggestions for improvement:

Video Practice Sessions

Inasmuch as we are beyond *Telling Ain't Training,* here is one more activity to help grow your own and your colleagues' training delivery competencies. We call this the Video Practice Session (VPS).

VPS provides simulated practice in training delivery. It offers trainer practice and feedback in a laboratory setting. In addition to written and oral feedback, trainers can take home their own personal videotapes to review—permanent records of their growing capabilities. The videotapes also help them set goals for future sessions.

Qualifications for Facilitating a VPS

It is extremely important that not just anyone conduct a VPS. The best facilitator for this is a master trainer who is very grounded in the principles of *Telling Ain't Training,* has experience training trainers, and stands out as a role model to others.

Facilities, Equipment, and Materials Required

We have found that seven is the maximum number of participants for a VPS. Five or six is ideal. You need a minimum room size of 15' x 20' for every seven participants in order to record the practice training sessions. The room should be equipped with eight chairs and three long tables. And for each room you must have the following equipment and supplies:

- one TV monitor
- one color TV camera with record and playback capabilities (preferably with a timer), positioned on a tripod
- appropriate cables, cords, and extension cords
- remote microphone, if available (if not, make sure that the camera picks up voices clearly at a distance)
- one videotape per participant
- one large screen at the front of the room
- one LCD projector (or overhead projector if your organization still uses these)
- two flipchart easels and paper pads
- broad felt-tip pens in assorted colors
- a pair of scissors and a roll of masking tape
- 10 sheets of lined paper for each participant
- two pencils for each participant
- one battery-operated, digital watch or stopwatch (especially important if the camera does not have a built-in timer)
- 14 copies of the VPS Observation Checklist (Worksheet 13-8, page 143) for each participant
- one copy of Worksheet 8-2: Training Session Planning Sheet Assessment (page 70 of this book) for each participant

Examine Figure 13-1 as we describe how to arrange the room for the VPS. Place the screen, flipchart easels, and projector at the front of the room. (Remember to test all of your equipment before the session.)

Figure 13-1: Suggested Room Arrangement for a Video Practice Session

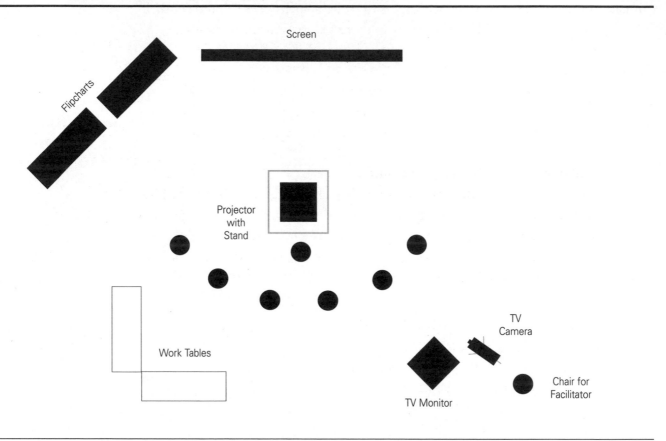

Create an informal training environment by arranging chairs in an open U-shape facing the screen. Use long tables to structure a U-shape, if desired. Place the camera (on a tripod) and the TV monitor at the back of the room. Position the camera to capture both the trainer and participants on tape. Position the TV monitor so that you can use it to monitor what you are taping. Make sure participants can't see the monitor screen because it can be distracting. During the feedback sessions, remember to put the camera lens cap on.

Test out your video equipment. Do a sound test. Use a remote microphone, if available. Turn the volume down as low as possible on the TV monitor to avoid a harsh screeching sound. (*Note:* If you do not know how to set up and/or test out the equipment, ask for technical assistance from someone who knows how to provide it.)

VPS Overview

15 minutes	**Introduction, Rationale, and Objectives**
45 minutes	**Preparation Period #1** *Participants prepare for their sessions.* *Facilitator circulates and provides feedback and support.*
10 minutes per participant	**Skill Practice #1 (with taping)** *Facilitator tapes participants in sequence on their own personal videotapes.*
15 minutes per participant	**Feedback Session #1** *After viewing each taping, everyone completes a VPS Observation Checklist (including the person whose session has just been viewed). Participants and facilitator then use the checklists in providing oral feedback to each taped participant.*
45 minutes	**Preparation Period #2** *Participants prepare for second practice session by reviewing the feedback they received on their first taped practice and making revisions to their presentations.* *Facilitator circulates and offers suggestions and support.*
10 minutes per participant	**Skill Practice #2 (with taping)** *Facilitator again tapes participants in sequence on participants' own tapes.*
15 minutes per participant	**Feedback Session #2** *Everyone completes a VPS Observation Checklist for each trainer, with special attention to the changes made following the first feedback session. Participants and facilitator again provide oral feedback to each trainer.*
15 minutes	**VPS Debriefing** *Facilitator and participants debrief the session.*
15 minutes	**Closing Remarks and Evaluation**

VPS Methodology

The VPS is designed to provide practice for and feedback to people who train others as part of their job. The VPS uses videotaped practice training sessions and feedback (both oral and written) as the primary instructional strategy.

There are no fixed criteria for success because each trainer brings to the VPS his or her own experience, strengths, and areas for improvement. The VPS enables each person to fine-tune his or her own skills. Participants should leave the VPS with increased competencies and confidence.

It is critical that the VPS facilitator create a supportive climate for the skill practice and feedback sessions. Emphasis should be placed on successful behaviors. Avoid criticism, sarcasm, or mockery of any kind. Also avoid sounding patronizing.

Research suggests that reinforcement of correct behaviors tends to improve them. Anything interpreted as a negative comment has unpredictable results. Research on what is called *autoscopy,* or viewing oneself, suggests that people who are videotaped performing a task are particularly vulnerable during playback. It's difficult to see oneself objectively. The subject tends to focus on negatives or weaknesses. Viewing himself or herself on the TV screen, especially with others in the room, can create anxiety. The VPS allows participants to take home their own personal videotapes so they can view in private or in the company of others after they have viewed them in the group.

VPS Introduction, Rationale, and Objectives. As with any meeting or training session, you will want to welcome the participants to the VPS and introduce yourself to the group. Ask your participants to introduce themselves and tell briefly what they hope to get out of the session. To put people more at ease and assure them that they are taking a risk for good reason, provide a solid rationale for participating in the VPS. Here is a sample script:

Rationale: Why Participate in the VPS?

Script: As trainers, we all want to perform well. We have all experienced poor training and want to avoid what is perceived as ineffective. The VPS offers you an opportunity to

- fine-tune skills
- see yourself as learners see you during training
- identify your strengths and the areas that need improvement
- practice training techniques in a safe, laboratory-type environment.

This VPS session has been designed with one overriding purpose: to help you in your training role.

The overall objective of the VPS is to help you run training sessions that

- are systematically designed
- include sound adult learning principles
- effectively attain their objectives
- are enjoyable both to the learners and to you.

Setting the Group at Ease Before and During the Taping. Training in front of a group of one's peers and being videotaped can cause nervousness or anxiety. Speaking in front of groups is most people's number-one fear. Couple this fact with capturing the performance on videotape and you have just raised the anxiety level several extra notches. Participants are vulnerable and may feel threatened by the experience. Therefore, you must position the practice sessions carefully. You will need to take a very positive and proactive approach to get the results you want to achieve. Above all, create a reassuring and supportive climate.

What follows are some tips to guide you in helping participants become comfortable before and during the VPS:

1. Select training topic assignments in advance of the session to give participants a reasonable amount of time to prepare and become comfortable with their content and training methodology. If projection visuals exist, show these to the participants. Provide electronic (on CDs) and paper copies of the visuals.

   Distribute a 10-minute section of the training program to each participant. Ask them to study their sections and prepare to present the content—adhering to the instructional design, but enhancing it with what they have learned from *Telling Ain't Training*.

   Note: If there are fewer than five participants, you may expand practice sessions to 15 minutes per trainer and adjust other timing accordingly.

2. Allow time for participants to prepare their sessions. Give the group approximately 45 minutes to prepare before being videotaped.

3. Circulate around the room during the preparation period. Review each person's training plan, reinforcing strengths and pointing out potential problems (such as not enough participant involvement, no means to verify learning, and so forth). Make suggestions and relieve concerns. Distribute copies of Worksheet 8-2 to the participants.

4. Before videotaping, explain the game plan to participants. Let them know that each of them will be videotaped. Their videotaping will be followed immediately by a feedback session. Share and explain the VPS Observation Checklist. The box below defines each item of the VPS Observation Checklist and the rating system. You can use these definitions as a script for acquainting participants with the checklist.

Rationale:	The trainer clearly established in a meaningful way the reason why the session was of benefit to the learners.
Objective(s):	The trainer clearly established what the learners would be able to do (the verifiable outcome for them) as a result of participating in the session.
Activities:	Learners were actively engaged throughout the session. The trainer continuously involved the learners in meaningful ways and drew from them to advance the session.
Evaluation:	The trainer verified learner progress through questions, exercises, or activities, and then verified to determine whether the learners attained the objective(s).
Feedback:	The trainer provided to the learners both corrective and confirming feedback that focused on their accomplishment of the objective(s). This was done in a positive and encouraging way.
Body language:	The trainer used body movement and gesture to convey a sense of openness and confidence. The use of the body was dynamic and communicated energy and enthusiasm.
Voice:	The trainer spoke clearly, energetically, and convincingly. The trainer conveyed enthusiasm for the session content and caring for learners to learn. The pace, tone, and volume varied to stimulate learner interest and sustain attention.
Eye contact:	The trainer kept his or her eyes on the learners almost all of the time, varying eye contact with each of the learners to draw and sustain attention. This was done in an open, nonthreatening way.

(continued on page 142)

(continued from page 141)

Preparation, organization, and time management:	The learning sequence of the session was logical and led the learners systematically to objective attainment. The use of time was efficient and effective. All materials and resources were available at the appropriate moment. The session flowed at a brisk but unhurried pace and was completed within the allotted time.
Visual aids:	Support materials were well designed, easy to understand, appropriate to the training, and reinforced (never competed with) the learning content and objective attainment.

Rating system:

Very good	The trainer met all of the criteria for the item.
Good	The trainer partially met the criteria for the item.
Needs Improvement	The trainer did not meet the criteria for the item. Either the trainer entirely missed the item or requires considerable practice to meet the criteria at a satisfactory level.

Prepare them for what everyone will be looking for in each session. Stress the importance of participant involvement and discourage one-way telling.

5. Check out equipment in advance. It's important that your equipment be ready to go when the group is ready. A delay at this point will raise anxiety levels and increase participant nervousness.

6. Ask for a volunteer to go first. Oftentimes, individuals who are particularly nervous will want to go first—to get it over with—so that they can then relax and enjoy the other training sessions. If no one volunteers, ask one of the most confident participants to lead off.

7. Explain the three-minute warning. Participants are often overly concerned about the short amount of time they have for their sessions. They express concern regardless of the length of time they have—15 minutes, 20 minutes, or more. To help them monitor their time, explain that you will hold up a "three minutes to go" sign to cue them when they are close to the end of their taping.

8. Start the applause after each taping. The group will join in, reinforcing the trainer and setting the stage for the feedback session.

9. Make a brief, positive statement after each training taping. Comments such as "nice job," "good work," or "you must be pleased with the way the session went" will make the trainer feel good and will encourage participants who are next in line.

Usually, following these pointers will put participants at ease. Occasionally, however, a participant will need more personal attention. Be sensitive to your learners' needs. Provide private coaching and reassurance, as required. Remember, however, you are not a therapist. You cannot be responsible for supplying self-esteem or overcoming a serious or persistent fear.

Advise the participants that their videotaped sessions will not be circulated. To ensure confidentiality, videotapes are labeled for each participant and given to them personally for their own viewing and use after the session is over.

Worksheet 13-8: VPS Observation Checklist

Trainer's Name: _____ Date: _____

	Very Good	Good	Needs Improvement
1. Rationale			
2. Objective(s)			
3. Activities			
4. Evaluation			
5. Feedback			
6. Body language			
7. Voice			
8. Eye contact			
9. Preparation, organization, and time management			
10. Visual aids			

Compliments: _____

_____

_____

Suggestions: _____

_____

_____

Skill Practice Training Sessions. Now let's review the steps to take in implementing a VPS:

1. Arrange visual aids on flipcharts in the same sequence as the trainers who will be conducting their practice sessions.[2] Participants may also provide handouts or use other materials or equipment during their sessions, as appropriate.
2. Ensure that learners have paper and pencils in case the trainer directs them to do written work.
3. Ask each trainer to prepare his or her learners by telling them where their segment fits into the overall course. Do not record this part of the session—it doesn't count within the time limits.
4. Time the session, beginning with a signal to the trainer that you are recording. Some video cameras have timers that can track time. If your equipment

does not have a timer, use a stopwatch, digital watch, or battery-operated timer. Because time management is one of the skills being evaluated, it is important to time the sessions accurately.

5. During the session, tape the trainer, the learners, the visual aids, and the activities. Start with a long shot to orient the session, setting, and learners. Then tighten the picture to focus on details such as hand gestures, visual aids, and learners' reactions. Professional or artistic filming techniques are not nearly as important as capturing interesting or important images and words that can make or reinforce a key point about training techniques that work, as well as those that don't.

6. Cue the trainer when there are three minutes to go. This should be done unobtrusively by raising the "three minutes to go" sign with your hand. However, trainers frequently get carried away with the session and totally forget you are there. If you feel the trainer may not see the warning sign, snap your fingers once to capture her or his attention as you raise the sign.

7. Close the session by starting a round of applause. As pointed out earlier, this is encouraging to trainer and learners alike.

8. Make a brief positive comment. Reinforce the trainer orally by saying something such as "nice job," "good work," or "you ought to feel good about that performance."

9. Ask the trainer to clear the training area for the next trainer—that is, remove or cover all visual aids that compete for attention. Remove the projector if it is not needed for the next person.

Feedback Sessions

1. Introduce the VPS Observation Checklist (Worksheet 13-8) and describe its use. Explain the rating plan, using a positive approach: "Ratings are either *very good, good,* or *needs improvement.* Check the appropriate box." Tell participants to write at least one positive comment in the *compliments* section and at least one prescriptive statement in the *suggestions* section. Explain that a prescriptive statement does not tell someone what they did wrong; rather, it offers constructive tips on how to overcome a problem or enhance an already satisfactory performance.

2. Explain how to give oral feedback. Explain that you will be calling on learners in random order, asking for a positive statement only from the learner's perspective about what they saw in the trainer's session. This is to create a positive reinforcing environment that focuses on successes. You will call on the trainer last and request a positive statement about his or her own session. You will also ask the trainer to offer a suggestion for improvement as if he or she were the trainer's supervisor. Finally, you will comment on the trainer's performance, summarizing the feedback from the group and adding a few comments of your own.

3. Give participants a couple of minutes to complete their VPS Observation Checklists for each trainer.

4. Randomly call on learners one at a time to make a positive statement about what they saw in the trainer's session. Call on the trainer last to comment on what he or she liked particularly in the session. Also ask the trainer for any suggestions for improving his or her performance (objectively, from the viewpoint of his or her supervisor).

5. Comment on the trainer's performance, summarizing the feedback from the group and adding a few comments of your own.

6. Collect the VPS Observation Checklists from each participant after each session.

7. Complete steps 3 through 6 after each trainer has been taped.

8. After all of the taping sessions, give each trainer the VPS Observation Checklists that you and each participant used to rate that trainer. Sign your own checklist. Other participant sheets remain anonymous.

9. Explain to participants that they are to review the feedback and use it to enhance their next practice session. The private reviewing of the suggestions reduces stress. Suggestions offered orally and in public can be perceived as criticism and may create unnecessary stress.

Trainer Skill Practice Debriefing. The purpose of the debriefing is to draw from the participants how they felt about the practice sessions as well as what they learned. Focus on using corrective feedback to improve and enhance performance. You can elicit useful information from participants by asking questions such as these:

1. Did you learn anything new about your training or yourself? If so, please explain.

2. Did you learn any new techniques or strategies as you watched others? If so, please explain.

3. What have you learned from this experience that you will keep as you prepare to deliver training sessions in the future? Please explain.

Closing Remarks and Trainer Skill Practice Evaluation. Bring the VPS to a close by congratulating all of the trainers on their enthusiastic involvement. Stress the changes and progress you have seen between the practice sessions. Reinforce the following key messages:

1. Adults learn best when they know *why* they are supposed to learn something. Provide a clear rationale, highlighting the benefits to them.

2. Adults learn best when they know *what* they are supposed to learn. Provide clear, comprehensible objectives stated in learner terms.

3. Adults learn best when they are actively engaged in learning activities. Make them do it!

4. Adults learn best when they are evaluated and either given corrective feedback—positively—or confirming feedback ("You got it!").

Remind the VPS participants that a polished presentation is not as important as being sensitive to learners and their learning needs. They should go for maximum learner involvement!

Answer any final questions. Wish them well, and tell them how and where they can receive additional support back on the job.

Form a *Telling Ain't Training* Study Group

Telling Ain't Training and the *Beyond Telling Ain't Training Fieldbook* are books to be *used*. One way of using them is by creating a study group. Have each person accept responsibility for leading a discussion about a chapter or topic. Create a calendar of meeting dates when the group will get together (live or virtually) to discuss what they read, tried, and discovered as they went through the assigned material. The discussions should include the following points:

♦ What are the key concepts, principles, or practices?
♦ How do these add value to learning? Performance? Our organization?
♦ What should we do with this information?
♦ What action plans can we create?
♦ How do we verify results?
♦ How do we obtain the required approvals and support?

These are suggested questions only . . . starting points for your group's ongoing growth and development.

Become a Learner Again

Taking classes or enrolling in a self-instructional course in an area unfamiliar to you can be a wonderful growth experience in two ways: You learn something new, and you relearn what it's like to be a learner. As a result, you receive valuable cues about what you should be doing in your training role. After a class or session, review what the trainer did, using the Trainer Observation and Feedback Form (Worksheet 13-7). For each item, ask yourself what you would have done—or how you might have improved performance. We take a least two courses a year on something, and we encourage you to do the same. Isn't there a saying about walking in another person's shoes. . . ?

Chapter Summary

What a well-packed chapter! Let's review what you experienced in it.

♦ You assessed yourself and your training organization again, just as you did in chapter 2 of this *Fieldbook*. Then you compared your perceptions of current and desired states for you and your training group then and now. That's food for thought and, we hope, encouragement.

◆ You visited the trainer's three Cs (competence, confidence, and caring), and discovered the importance of these for effective training and for ongoing growth and development.

◆ You reflected on how to build a support system for yourself and as a group with your fellow trainers. You generated actions in both cases and created action plans for making these happen.

◆ You identified factors in your environment that either facilitate or inhibit your moving to your desired training states. Once again you created action plans, this time to enhance the facilitating factors and decrease or eliminate the inhibitors.

◆ You learned to use a Trainer Observation and Feedback Form to promote ongoing improvement in training delivery.

◆ You received a detailed plan for developing video practice sessions to build training competencies.

◆ You considered suggestions for setting up a *Telling Ain't Training* study group and periodically becoming a learner.

This was a substantial chapter because it included what to do when you leave us. There is always a flurry of activities when people are getting ready to say farewell. We leave you here with one last action item. Review this chapter a second time very soon. Select from it what you can do for ongoing growth and development for yourself and your colleagues. Set things in motion quickly because inertia will work against you as will the temptation to maintain the status quo. Organize with your teammates. Get your management onboard. Use the tools and suggestions in this chapter and the next one to create the professional learning and performance support team you believe in.

Notes

1. State of the Industry 2004: ASTD's Annual Review of Trends in Workplace Learning and Performance, by B. Sugrue and K. Kyung-Hyun (Alexandria, VA: ASTD Press).

2. If the participant has prepared projection visuals, load these to a single LCD projector and test them. Otherwise, recommend using flipchart visuals for practice.

Chapter 14

External Support Systems

This chapter

- examines ways the external world beyond your training organization can assist you in reaching new training heights
- explains the value of joining local or industry-based training associations
- suggests benefits to you for joining national and international training or performance improvement societies
- describes value to be gained from attending workshops and training conferences and from forming relationships with colleges and universities
- encourages you to read professionally in the field and gives you some excellent starting places to explore
- lays out the benefits of networking
- welcomes you to continue the dialogue with the authors.

This final chapter adds an external dimension for supporting your ongoing progress toward becoming a *Telling Ain't Training* organization—one that achieves the learner transformations that lead to valued results for all. The first recommendation we offer is our strongest one: Become active professionally outside of your company.

Join a Local or Industry-Based Training Association

We suggested in the previous chapter that joining a training society offers self-development benefits. We return to this and add that being part of such a group provides an external support system for you and your training organization. Such groups

- share best practices
- obtain speakers at a much lower cost than your own training organization would have to pay
- keep members current on what is happening in the field

- provide collegiality when support is needed
- act as a sounding board for your issues, concerns, and ideas
- usually give out awards for member (individual and organizational) accomplishments, which reinforces, validates, and enhances your and your team's efforts
- offer an opportunity for networking, which leads to recruitment of talent, hiring of consultants and freelancers, and to possibilities for your own future career moves.

These associations can be local, with members representing a wide range of industries. This type of diversity encourages cross-pollination of ideas. Industry-based training associations offer the advantage of focusing on concerns similar to those of your own training organization. Training associations exist in the pharmaceutical, financial, railway, high-technology, telecom, and many other industries.

An Activity for You

Contact your local chamber of commerce to identify training associations in your area. Also, contact the American Society for Training & Development (ASTD) at www.astd.org, the Canadian Society for Training and Development (CSTD) at www.cstd.ca, or the International Society for Performance Improvement (ISPI) at www.ispi.org for information on local chapters in your geographic region. (ASTD and ISPI also have chapters in many other countries.) For industry groups, the best way to start is with an Internet search. We typed into a search engine *training association* and several different industries (for example, construction, banking, railway, waste management), and in every case we discovered a broad array of professional support groups.

An Activity for Your Training Organization

Create a list of potential local associations to explore. Gather information and set up a file on each one. Circulate these files to your training colleagues. Hold a meeting to discuss impressions and reactions. Assign individuals to explore further and report back. Finally, select a local and/or industry training association in which to become active. If the association has the potential to support your training organization, not only become active, but also accept increasing leadership positions. You will grow individually and your training organization will reap the rewards of your expanding vision and capabilities.

Join a National or International Training or Performance Improvement Society

We have already mentioned ASTD, CSTD, and ISPI. These associations produce publications and reports that are of immense benefit to training professionals. Their fees are reasonable. Their conferences, along with VNU Learning's Training Conference and Training Directors Forum, are extremely professional and provide continuing learning opportunities for you and your team. They also offer certificate programs to enhance performance capabilities in a variety of training-relevant areas.

Attend Workshops and Training Conference Events

There are dangers in becoming too internally fixated on your work. Attending local and national workshops and conferences opens one's eyes to new possibilities. Often the materials from these events can constitute the basis for significant change in your work setting. We recommend getting on email lists from ASTD, CSTD, ISPI, training, and industry/local associations. Training periodicals also announce learning and conference events. Webinars are a growing vehicle for training professionals. Their advantage is that you need not travel to learn from external courses. Fees are generally low and the quality is becoming better as Webinar software becomes easier to use and more sophisticated in its interaction and delivery.

Create Relationships With Colleges and Universities

Educational institutions possess large amounts of expertise and resources that can augment the capacity of your training output at costs that are often less than your internal ones. Your local college or university may have software specialists and studios with which you can contract to develop and deliver Web-based learning and performance support. Subject-matter experts can help enhance content. Students, acting as interns, can increase your ability to undertake projects for which you have insufficient resources. You also contribute to the students' learning. Often, an intern becomes a potential recruit for your team.

Read

Build your knowledge of the training field and gain tools for improving your training organization's performance by reading books and periodicals on topics relevant to training.

Telling Ain't Training contains a large reading resource section. Beyond that list there is a huge number of reading materials, far too numerous to cite here. As training, learning, and human performance support continue to grow in importance, books and magazines are multiplying exponentially. Below is a list of publishers that specialize in these topical areas. We recommend that you research the following:

- ASTD Press—http://www.astd.org/astd/Publications/books/astd_press_books.htm
- ISPI—http://performance.ispi.org/source/library/ordershome.cfm?section=orders
- HRD Press—http://www.business-marketing.com/store/hrd.html
- Pfeiffer—http://www.pfeiffer.com/WileyCDA/Section/id-101552.html

- Berrett-Koehler—http://www.bkconnection.com/
- CEP Press—http://www.cepworldwide.com/storefront.asp

With respect to training magazines, we recommend

- *T+D* (ASTD's monthly magazine)—http://www.astd.org/astd/publications/td_magazine
- *Infoline* (ASTD's series of tips and tools)—http://www.astd.org/astd/publications/infoline/infoline_home
- *Training*—http://www.trainingmag.com
- *Performance Improvement Journal* (ISPI's monthly journal)—http://www.ispi.org/
- *Performance Improvement Quarterly* (ISPI's quarterly academic publication)—http://www.ispi.org/
- *Educational Technology Research and Development* (Association for Educational Communications and Technology's research quarterly)—http://www.aect.org/Intranet/Publications/index.asp

Build a Network

Local and industry associations are certainly excellent means for creating professional networks. Beyond these, we recommend searching your own organization for kindred spirits who believe that developing people is a worthwhile mission. Where do you find them? Almost anywhere. Here, however, is a high-probability starter list:

- human resources (especially if there is a human resource development group)
- other training groups in your organization (for example, information technology, sales, manufacturing, safety)
- individual contributors who occasionally train
- organizational development/organizational effectiveness specialists
- human factors/ergonomics specialists.

Brainstorm with your group to identify internal network contacts of value to or in support of the directions you wish to take in training. Include key influencers, informal leaders, union leaders, and managers who may champion your cause.

Outside of your training organization are like-minded thinkers in your industry, local training professionals, and national/international thought leaders. Most are open to exchanges of information. Exploit all of these potential links.

Stay in Touch

This brings us to the end of the *Beyond Telling Ain't Training Fieldbook,* but not to the conclusion of the dialogue we have established with you. We are always open to chat and help support you. We simply say here, "Auf wiedersehen," which means until we see each other again. Our Website is www.hsa-lps.com. There you can find free articles to download and an e-newsletter you can receive online at no cost.

This *Fieldbook* is a tool-based resource for you. *Use it.* Build your and your training organization's capability and strength. Let us know how you are doing. Our best wishes for success go with you.

About the Authors

Harold D. Stolovitch and **Erica J. Keeps** share a common passion—developing people. Together they have devoted a combined total of more than 70 years to make workplace learning and performance both enjoyable and effective. Their research and consulting activities have involved them in numerous projects with major corporations, such as Alcan, BBDO Detroit, Canadian Pacific Railway, The Coffee Bean & Tea Leaf, DaimlerChrysler Academy, General Motors, Hewlett-Packard, Prudential, and Sun Microsystems. Their dedication to improving workplace learning and performance is reflected in the workshops they run internationally—workshops that focus on training delivery, instructional design, and performance consulting. Stolovitch and Keeps are the principals of HSA LEARNING & PERFORMANCE SOLUTIONS LLC, specialists in the application of instructional technology and human performance technology to business, industry, government, and the military. Together, they are co-editors of both editions of the award-winning *Handbook of Human Performance Technology: A Comprehensive Guide for Analyzing and Solving Performance Problems in Organizations* and *Improving Individual and Organizational Performance Worldwide* published by Jossey-Bass/Pfeiffer. They are also the authors of the award-winning best sellers *Telling Ain't Training* and *Training Ain't Performance*, published by ASTD. Stolovitch and Keeps are co-editors and co-authors of the *Learning & Performance Toolkit* series published by Pfeiffer.

Harold D. Stolovitch, CPT, is a graduate of both McGill University (Montreal) and Indiana University (Bloomington), where he completed a PhD and post-doctoral work in instructional systems technology. With one foot solidly grounded in the academic world and the other in the workplace, Stolovitch has conducted a large number of research studies and practical projects aimed at achieving high learning and performance results. In addition to creating countless instructional materials for a broad range of work settings, he has authored almost 200 articles, research reports, book chapters, and books. He is a past president of the International Society for

Performance Improvement (ISPI), former editor of the *Performance Improvement Journal,* and editorial board member for several human resource and performance technology journals. He has won numerous awards throughout his 44-year career, including the Thomas F. Gilbert Award for Distinguished Professional Achievement; ISPI's highest honor, Member-for-Life; ASTD's 2003 Research Award; and the Canadian Society for Training and Development's most prestigious President's Award for lifetime contributions to the field. Stolovitch is an emeritus professor, Université de Montréal, where he headed the instructional and performance technology programs and a former clinical professor of human performance at work, University of Southern California.

Erica J. Keeps, CPT, holds a master's degree in educational psychology from Wayne State University (Detroit) and a bachelor's degree from the University of Michigan (Ann Arbor), where she later became a faculty member in the Graduate Business School Executive Education Center. Her 34-year professional career has included training management positions with J. L. Hudson Co. and Allied Supermarkets. She has consulted with a wide variety of organizations in the areas of learning and performance. Keeps has not only produced and supervised the production of numerous instructional materials and performance management systems but has also published extensively on the topic of improving workplace learning and performance. She has provided staff development for instructional designers, training administrators, and performance consultants. Keeps has been acknowledged by many learning and performance leaders as a caring mentor and major influence in their careers. She is a former executive board member of ISPI, a past president of the Michigan Chapter of ISPI, and a Member-for-Life of both the Michigan and Montreal ISPI chapters. Among her myriad awards for outstanding contributions to instructional and performance technology is ISPI's Distinguished Service Award for her many leadership roles.

The authors reside in Los Angeles and can be reached through their Website, www.hsa-lps.com.